SRA Read to Achieve

Comprehending
Narrative Text

Above and Beyond:
A Nonfiction Anthology

Nancy Marchand-Martella

Ronald Martella

Mc
Graw
Hill
Education

Acknowledgments

The authors thank Laura Apol, Ph.D., for her contribution in the selection of the literature for this anthology.

Grateful acknowledgment is given to the following publishers and copyright owners for permissions granted to reprint selections from their publications. All possible care has been taken to trace ownership and secure permission for each selection included. In case of any errors or omissions, the Publisher will be pleased to make suitable acknowledgments in future editions.

From NO END IN SIGHT by Rachael Scdoris. Copyright © 2005 by the author and reprinted by permission of St. Martin's Press, LLC.

Reprinted with permission for the book TRIAL BY ICE: A PHOTOBIOGRAPHY OF SIR ERNEST SHACKLETON by K.M. Kostyal. Copyright © 1999 National Geographic Society.

PRINCESS OF THE PRESS: The Story of Ida B. Wells-Barnett by Angela Shelf Medearis. Copyright © 1997 by Angela Shelf Medearis. All rights reserved including the right of reproduction in whole or in part in any form. This edition published by arrangement with Dutton Children's Books, a member of Penguin Young Readers Group, a division of Penguin Group (USA) Inc.

PHINEAS GAGE: A Gruesome but True Story About Brain Science by John Fleischman. Copyright © 2002 by John Fleischman. Reprinted by permission of Houghton Mifflin Company. All rights reserved.

mheducation.com/prek-12

Send all inquiries to:
McGraw-Hill Education
8787 Orion Place
Columbus, OH 43240

ISBN: 978-0-07-622000-7
MHID: 0-07-622000-1

Printed in the United States of America.

9 10 11 12 13 QVS 22 21 20 19 18

ABOVE AND BEYOND

A Nonfiction Anthology

No End in Sight

Trial by Ice:

A Photobiography of Sir Ernest Shackleton

Princess of the Press:

The Story of Ida B. Wells-Barnett

Phineas Gage:

A Gruesome but True Story About Brain Science

Contents

No End in Sight   6

Beyond the Book:

TRIAL BY ICE: 44
A Photobiography of Sir Ernest Shackleton

Beyond the Book:

Contents

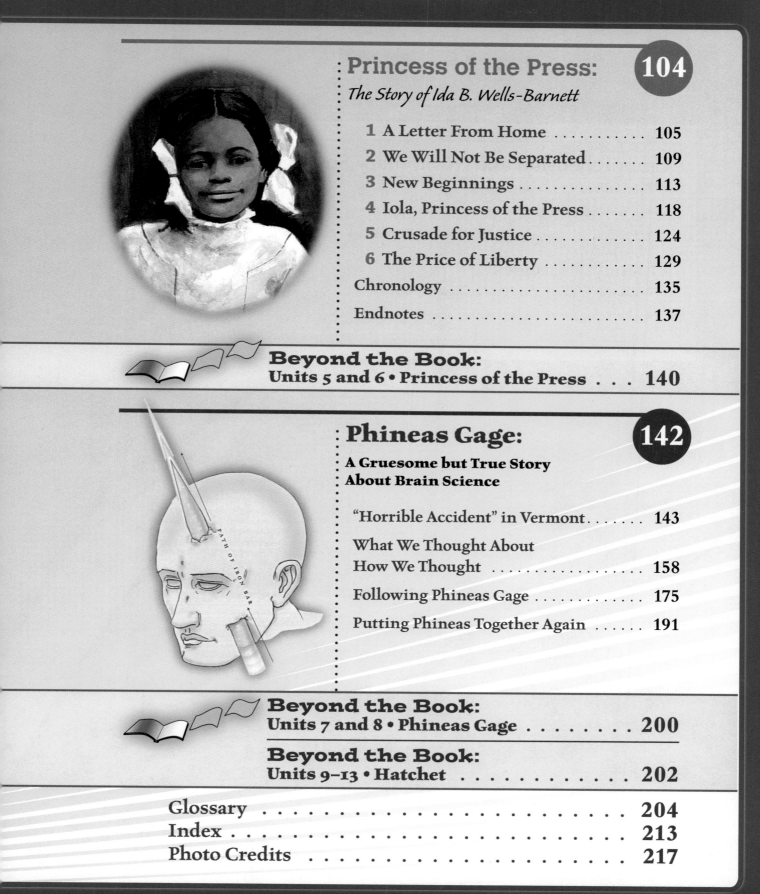

Tools for Reading

1 Above and Beyond: A Nonfiction Anthology and Hatchet

Comprehension and Vocabulary Strategies
- *Identify story structure.*
- *Use mental imagery.*
- *Predict, question, clarify, and summarize text.*

Fluency Strategies
- *Develop reading speed and accuracy.*
- *Develop a better understanding of what you read.*

2 Beyond the Book

Application of Skills

Improve your understanding of other informational text. Use research strategies to learn more about topics of interest after you read sources such as newspapers, magazines, Web sites, brochures, and menus. Extend your learning with a written response.

3 Teacher-Selected Book

Before You Read

Use strategies you've learned before you read a chapter or section of a book.

As You Read

Use strategies you've learned as you read a chapter or section of a book.

After You Read

Use strategies you've learned after you read a chapter or section of a book.

Program Objectives

In this program, students will learn to use the following strategies:

	Comprehension and Vocabulary Strategies	Unit range
1	**Identify** story structure such as characters, setting, plot, and other story components (i.e., author, illustrator, genre, theme, perspective, mood, and author's purpose).	1–15
2	**Use** mental imagery to visualize characters, settings, and plot.	1–15
3	**Preview** narrative text.	3–15
4	**Read** narrative text with a clearly established purpose.	3–15
5	**Use** background knowledge on specified topics.	3–15
6	**Make** predictions, and verify them.	3–15
7	**Generate** literal and inferential questions.	4–15
8	**Monitor** comprehension, including rereading and adjusting reading rate.	5–15
9	**Use** strategies to decode multipart words.	5–15
10	**Use** context clues to determine unfamiliar word meaning.	5–15
11	**Use** a glossary to determine unfamiliar word meaning.	5–15
12	**Use** a dictionary to determine unfamiliar word meaning.	5–15
13	**Use** a computer to determine unfamiliar word meaning.	5–15
14	**Retell** what is happening in a story.	6–15
15	**Summarize** what was read by developing a gist.	6–15

Comprehension and Vocabulary Strategies		Unit range
16	**Use** pre-, during-, and post-reading strategies to improve text understanding.	3–15
17	**Use** graphic organizers to keep track of important information.	1–15
18	**Use** strategies such as PQCS to organize information and to gain meaning from text.	3–15
19	**Collaborate** with peers in a reciprocal-teaching format.	9–15

Higher-Order Thinking Skills		Unit range
20	**Answer** questions aligned with all levels of Bloom's Taxonomy.	1–15
21	**Answer** standardized-test questions.	1–15
22	**Use** graphic organizers to track important information.	1–15
23	**Use** metacognitive strategies to select strategies, and explain why you chose them.	1–15

Fluency Strategies		Unit range
24	**Read** narrative text fluently using repeated reading techniques.	1–15
25	**Use** various practice activities, such as oral, shared, and silent reading, to improve fluency and reading for meaning.	1–15

No End in Sight

My Life as a Blind Iditarod Racer

Rachael Scdoris and Rick Steber

A BEAUTIFUL BABY

Background Information

Rachael Scdoris wanted to become one of the best professional sled-dog racers in the world, but she had a visual impairment. She did not want to be thought of as disabled but rather as someone who saw things differently than others saw them.

I was born February 1, 1985, the same year Libby Riddles became the first woman to win the Iditarod. According to my parents, I was an incredibly beautiful baby, but, of course, all parents say that. I was nearly a month late and had to be taken by cesarean section. I weighed ten pounds, eight ounces, measured twenty-four inches, and was the largest girl baby born up to that time at St. Charles Hospital in Bend, Oregon. I came into this world with a full head of blond hair.

Since I was too young to know what was going on during that time, I have relied on what my father, Jerry, and mother, Lisa, have told me about this period of my life. According to Dad, within a few days of bringing me home he began to notice something abnormal about my eyes. When he held me close and cooed to me, he said I was not able to focus on his face. It was as if I was searching for the source of the sound but unable to locate it.

Dad actually returned to the hospital and asked one of the nurses in Pediatrics about his concern. She told him, "It's not uncommon. It takes some babies a few weeks, or even a month, to be able to focus. Don't worry." She showed him other newborns, and when a few did not look directly at him when he spoke this seemed to put his mind at ease, at least for a while.

My parents claim I was an easy baby to care for, that I slept when I was supposed to sleep and rarely cried unless I was hungry or needed my diaper changed. But Dad was plagued by what he perceived to be a problem with my eyes. The day I turned one month old he called the doctor and said, "Something is definitely wrong with her vision."

"Each baby develops differently, at his or her own pace. There is nothing to be concerned about," the doctor reassured him.

"No, you don't understand. Her eyesight isn't normal," Dad insisted.

"Mr. Scdoris, your baby is developing. It just takes time. Give it a few months," the doctor said.

My condition never changed. And while Dad was adamant that I had a problem, Mom was more patient and accepting. She thought I was flawless in every way.

"Come over here," Dad told Mom one evening. He was holding me in his arms. "Say something to Rachael and watch her eyes."

"Hey, pretty girl. How's my pretty baby?" Mom babbled. I turned my head searching, even grinned at her, but my eyes never found her.

"See that. She hears perfectly but her eyes can't find you," Dad said.

Having heard this same discourse for the past four months, Mom lost her patience and said, "Okay, tomorrow I'll schedule an appointment with Dr. Berube. We'll get to the bottom of this. He can run tests or whatever he has to do. Promise me one thing: If he says Rachael is fine, I don't want to hear another word out of you. Agree?"

"Fine," Dad told her.

That appointment proved to be the first of an endless string of appointments at doctors' offices. When we met with Dr. Stacy Berube at Central Oregon Pediatric Associates, Dad told him, "Please don't placate me and tell me she is just slow developing her eyesight. Something is definitely wrong."

"Describe the problem she is having," Dr. Berube said.

"I'll show you," said Dad. He went through what he later described as his little dog and pony show, speaking to me and me not looking directly at him. He had Mom do the same thing.

The doctor used a pencil-thin instrument with a light on one end to peer into my eyes. Then, without saying anything to my parents, he walked out of the room and returned with another doctor. This doctor went through the same procedure. The two of them stepped into the hallway and conversed in muffled voices. When Dr. Berube returned to the room he said, "I can tell you this right now, so you no longer have to worry needlessly. . . ."

Dad claimed a wave of relief swept over him because, for an instant, he believed I was fine. That he had been wrong. That everyone else was right. My eyesight was fine, just slow developing. And then Dr. Berube dropped the bombshell.

"I don't believe she is totally blind. She may be partially sighted."

After that announcement, life would never again be the same for any of us in the Scdoris family. Dad, in a state of shock, responded with anger. "What are you talking about? My baby's not blind."

Dad told me that at that moment he felt as though he were back playing football at David Douglas High School and some 250-pound lineman had blindsided him. It was difficult for him to breathe. He could not say anything else.

"What does that mean?" Mom asked.

"At this point I'm not totally sure," Dr. Berube said. "I want Rachael to see Dr. East. He's an ophthalmologist. His office is just up the street. If it's all right with you, I'll call and see if we can come up."

"I don't think we ought to be in a rush. We've already waited four months. Maybe we can come in next week. I really don't want to do this right now." Dad was in denial. He did not want an ophthalmologist to confirm that his daughter was nearly blind.

Dr. Berube was gentle but firm. "This needs to be done immediately. I would like for an ophthalmologist to substantiate what I found. Perhaps there is some treatment available for your daughter." He made the call, hung up the phone, swept me up, and carried me in his arms the short half block to Dr. East's office. My dazed parents trailed behind like sad afterthoughts.

Dr. Sam East had Dad sit in a chair and hold me while he conducted a comprehensive examination of my eyes. When he finished he turned his attention to my parents and told them, "I detected limited vision and estimate your baby has eyesight no better than 20-200."

"What does that mean?" Dad wanted to know.

"She is most probably in the category of legally blind."

"Whoa, just a minute. Legally blind? What are you talking about?" Dad cried.

Dr. East gave an audible sigh. "When she is older she may be able to function normally, but she will always require special accommodations."

Dad claimed a thousand thoughts were racing through his mind. He wanted to know what the doctor meant by the words "special accommodations." He wanted out of the room. He wanted to go back in time, to when he only suspected something was wrong, before it had become a medical certainty. He wanted me to be healthy and normal, his perfect baby girl. He mumbled, "I don't want this thing."

"I know you don't. None of us do," Dr. East said.

"Is it correctable? Can't she just wear glasses?" Mom asked.

"At this point we don't know, not without further testing."

"It won't get any worse, will it?" Mom asked.

"It's impossible to tell," the doctor said, and then, searching to soften his diagnosis, he added, "We hope it doesn't."

My parents were totally devastated by the news their baby was legally blind. I've always had a nagging suspicion that at the moment the doctors gave my parents the news a tiny fissure began to form between them. In time it split them apart. I don't know if that is true or not, but I don't think the news helped bond them together. Little by little they grew apart, and when I was three years old they divorced and went their separate ways.

I lived with Dad. We had a cabin in the woods, ten miles from the town of Sisters and five miles from the nearest paved road. I still remember the house perched on top of a hill facing west, overlooking the beautiful panorama of the Cascade mountain range. Even I could see the mountains. The sharp, snowcapped peaks of the Three Sisters seemed close enough to reach out and touch.

Dad was a sled dog musher. As a boy he had fallen in love with the *Sergeant Preston of the Yukon* television show. He would pretend he was Sergeant Preston and run around calling out, "On, King, on you huskies. Mush!"

Sled dogs were nothing more than a child's fantasy until Dad went into the Army during the Vietnam War. Several Indians from Alaska were in his unit and he talked to them about sled dogs. Before snow machines became popular, everyone in the North drove dogs. It was a way of life in those days.

When Dad was discharged from the Army in 1970 it was his dream to settle in Alaska, file on a homestead, and put together a team of dogs. But instead he enrolled in college and graduated with a degree in education. His first job was teaching at Gold Beach on the Oregon coast. Here he met a fellow from North Bend who was training sled dogs with a cart on the beach. Shortly after that encounter Dad got his first sled dog, Jenny. Within a couple years he had seven dogs.

In 1978 he ran the Sisters Sled Dog Race, and according to the story that he loves to tell, it was one of those magical nights, ten below zero, the moon was out, and it was snowing. It was so perfect that right then and there, he made up his mind what he wanted to do with his life. He returned to Gold Beach and quit his job—although he honored his contract and finished out the year—and moved to Central Oregon to train and raise dogs.

Some of my earliest memories are of our little cabin on the top of the hill, surrounded by thirty-two dogs chained to stakes driven into the ground. Each dog had his own individual doghouse. I played with the puppies and helped Dad feed and water the dogs and do cleanup chores.

The year I was born Dad had acquired a sled dog sponsor, Elliott Dog Food. They were in the process of developing a complete nutritional formula for working dogs and used our kennel to conduct research. Dad trained dogs, competed in sled dog races throughout the Northwest, and made public appearances to promote Elliott Dog Food. I went everywhere with him. On training runs Dad tied my car seat onto the basket on the sled and slipped dog booties on my hands as mittens. I was happy as could be. But I cannot remember much about the rides, because as soon as we started on the big loop that wound around through the forest I fell asleep. I'm not sure why; maybe what made me drowsy was the motion of the sled or the feeling of speed, or perhaps I just felt sheltered and secure.

Sometimes I spent weekends with Mom, but usually I was with Dad at the cabin. And there were the trips we took back and forth to Portland. We made a lot of trips to Portland, meeting with doctors at Oregon Health & Science University and Devers Memorial Eye Clinic. One of the leading retinal specialists in the world, Dr. Richard Weleber, a professor of ophthalmology and medical genetics with a specialty in congenital and hereditary eye diseases at the OHSU Casey Eye Institute, took a special interest in me. He tested, retested, and tested me some more.

For a time we worked with two researchers who were conducting post-doctoral work in the field of genetics. They wanted to know about our family history, if there had ever been any member of our family who had been blind or had vision problems. Dad and Mom tried to trace their genealogy, but it seems as if our ancestors were mostly farmers or common laborers, and if they had had problems with their vision it was never noted.

Dad had accepted the clinical diagnosis, that I was legally blind, but what he kept trying to find out from Dr. Weleber was what, as a father, should he do? How could he help me? Would I have trouble interacting and socializing with other children? Would I ever be able to take care of myself, hold a job, and lead a normal life? What could he do to help me prepare for adulthood? How could he make my life easier and more fulfilling?

Dr. Weleber would shrug his shoulders. "I don't know."

Dad would press him for information. "Will she be able to learn? Will she have to read Braille? Will her classmates accept her?"

"I'm a doctor. I'm a scientist. I specialize on what is inside the eye. Beyond that, I do not know about such things."

It seemed that every specialist who looked at my eyes gave me another prescription for eyeglasses. I was only nine months old when I was fitted with my first pair of glasses. We have pictures of me, this little baby wearing glasses with lenses as thick as a Coke bottle.

The first glasses I remember were pink. That was my favorite color at the time and they had the image of Minnie Mouse on each corner of the frames. I was constantly taking off my glasses, laying them down, and losing them. Anyway, they were not very effective in helping me see, and I stopped the charade of wearing them when kids my age began teasing me.

Even though we continued to make regular visits to Portland, the doctors were unable to determine a diagnosis. Finally we received a partial answer, or at least a postponed possible answer. Dr. Weleber said that when I turned six years old I would be able to respond to cognitive questions. He promised that at that point he could make a definitive diagnosis. And so we went home and waited.

During this interval Dad was forced to make one of the most difficult and heart-wrenching decisions of his life. He came to the conclusion that living out rural like we did was not in my best interests, that I needed to have a more traditional home environment near kids my own age, and that we should live close enough to town to take advantage of the various state and federal programs available to blind children.

Dad made two telephone calls. One was to Jeffrey Mann in Alaska and the other to John Patten in Minnesota. Both were close friends and fellow mushers. Dad put it to them straight: "I need a favor. I want you to come get my dogs."

They dropped everything and came as quickly as they could. Neither stayed very long. They just loaded up the dogs and departed.

I recently asked Dad about that day, because I do not remember anything about what happened. I just came home and found the dogs were gone. Dad confessed he had sent me away to stay with friends. He was trying to protect me.

I picture Dad loving the dogs, saying his good-byes to Lester, Jagger, Nellie, Mickey, and all the rest, standing there alone, watching his dogs and his way of life going off down the road. He said when the trucks, with his dogs inside the dog box, pulled away from the cabin he stood there watching their progress toward the highway by the dust trail that rose and floated above the tops of the trees. And he cried.

He gave up everything for me. I genuinely admire and have the deepest respect for Dad, that he was willing to make such an enormous sacrifice for me. Those dogs were almost like children to him. They were some of the finest sled dogs in the world. In fact, John Patten took a team of dogs that included many of Dad's dogs to Alaska and raced the Iditarod in 1988. He finished eighteenth, which at that time was the second-highest finish for a team made up of dogs from the Lower 48.

By giving away his dogs Dad had put my welfare above the way of life he had chosen and enjoyed so much. He set aside his personal dreams, his wants and desires, for me. I think that is the genuine measure of love, real true love.

THE DIAGNOSIS

Background Information

Rachael moved to Bend, Oregon, with her father, who signed her up for mobility training. Rachael learned to use a black-and-white cane she named Moo-Moo Cow. Later people made fun of her cane, and she never used it again.

Shortly after my sixth birthday we visited Dr. Weleber in Portland. I was taken to an examination room and helped into an enormous chair. The armrests were so tall that when I placed my elbows on them my shoulders shrugged up around my ears. There was not so much as a pinprick of light entering this room. I felt claustrophobic and had an unreasonable fear that if I should try to breathe too deeply I might suck the blackness into my lungs and suffocate.

Dad was in the room with me. Knowing he was there reassured me, but still I felt alone and vulnerable. A bad thing could happen and Daddy would not be able to find me in the dark. Any old monster could be lurking in the evil darkness. I squirmed in the leather chair and could feel the bottom of the headrest touching the top of my head. I had a suspicion the chair might try to swallow me.

"Daddy." My voice seemed puny in all the blackness.

"I'm right here, sweetie," he called. His voice was strong and reassuring. It helped to bolster me.

"Daddy, do you want to sing with me?"

"Sure. What do you want to sing?"

At that time I was obsessed with *The Sound of Music.* I was constantly playing the sound track. We sang "Do-Re-Mi" and "My Favorite Things," and we sang "Climb Every Mountain." As our voices blended together the blackness was not nearly so oppressive.

I don't know how he found his way into and across the room, but Dr. Weleber was suddenly there, standing next to me.

"How are we doing today, young lady?"

"Fine," my voice squeaked.

Someone else was in the room, and from the lightness of the footsteps I assumed this other person was a woman. Dr. Weleber spoke, saying they were going to administer a series of tests. "Relax," he directed. He said it would take only a few minutes. I felt hands on my head and fingers probing here and there. I think they applied some type of goop and then fastened tiny suction cups to my scalp with wires running from them. I knew about the cups and wires because I reached up and felt one of them. An apparatus was fitted over my head. Dr. Weleber called it a spaceman's helmet. That made it fun. I fantasized I was a spaceman floating in the black void of the universe.

After handing me a handheld device and instructing me how to push a button in the center, the doctor and his assistant exited the room. I was left with Dad, out there somewhere, and the raspy sound of my own breathing.

I was thinking that I wanted to scratch my scalp and was wondering how I could go about it when a small light exploded in front of my eyes. It was like a tiny star exploding. This was followed by more bursts of light.

"When you see the color red, push the button," Dr. Weleber's voice commanded.

I saw a red light, pushed the button, and Dr. Weleber asked me to describe where, in my field of vision, I had seen it. And then I was supposed to respond to other colors when I saw them. It was wonderful, incredible, mind-boggling, this show of pulsating lights that sparkled, twinkled brightly, and winked out. For the first time in my life I witnessed the entire spectrum of color as though it were a sparkling rainbow painted across a galaxy of shooting stars. The vivid images of light and color burned into my retina and into my mind.

All too quickly the test was concluded and the overhead fluorescent lights were flipped on. The harshness of these lights gave me an instant headache, a headache so acute I thought I was going to be sick to my stomach. The space-man's helmet was removed and they pulled off the electrodes and tried to wipe away the goop that had affixed them to my scalp.

When Dad and I left the office that day we still did not have any answers about a diagnosis of my visual problems. Dr. Weleber sent us home with a single request: "Can you come back next week? We will have the results of the tests by then."

After years of waiting, Dr. Weleber had a definitive answer. We met him in his office the following week and he did not waste time on idle chitchat or pre-paring us for the results. The minute he entered the room he started talking.

"Without a doubt Rachael has a rare disease called congenital achromatopsia. It causes nearsightedness, farsightedness, and color blindness."

Dad wanted to know, "What can we do about it? Is there a cure?"

"As I said, this condition is extremely rare," explained Dr. Weleber. "It was only discovered in the past couple decades. Fewer than one hundred people have been diagnosed. We estimate about one out of every one hundred and eighty thousand people in the world will be stricken with congenital achromatopsia."

Mom was with us that day and she asked, "How did she get it?"

Dr. Weleber was blunt. "Congenital achromatopsia is a genetic condition and both parents must have recessive genes to pass it on to their offspring."

"Will she get better?" Dad asked.

"To be frank, we know very little about congenital achromatopsia. But I can tell you we believe the eyesight she has is stable. But anyone stricken with this condition is susceptible to any, and every, change in light conditions. Tracing past history of patients diagnosed with congenital achromatopsia, we find nearly all have complained that teachers, employers, and even spouses have accused them of faking their lack of vision. Most individuals report they have suffered socially, academically, and financially. We have only scratched the sur-face of researching and learning about this particular condition."

"What can we do?" Mom asked.

Dr. Weleber shrugged his shoulders. "Sunglasses might help, but only so much."

Dad came upright in his chair. "Sunglasses? That's all you have to offer? Sun-glasses?"

"I'm afraid so," Dr. Weleber stated.

We had waited six years for a diagnosis, and now that we had an answer Dad wanted to know, "Can you tell me how this is going to impact Rachael?"

"No. That is beyond the scope of my knowledge. I know about the science of retinal diseases. I do not know about the social implications. But there are other people who can help to answer your questions."

Dad was trying to wrap his mind around everything that had transpired and gauge what the future might hold. "So you're basically saying Rachael will just have to adjust to being blind?"

"Precisely. And now that we have made the diagnosis there is nothing more that we can do here at OHSU. But rest assured, if there are any scientific developments you will be notified. And of course, it goes without saying, if your daughter has any significant change with her vision, which we do not anticipate, please advise us immediately."

With that said, Dr. Weleber stood, shook hands with Dad and then Mom, patted me on the top of the head, and, as he walked from the room, tossed over his shoulder, "Well, good luck and good-bye."

And then he was gone. My parents sat for a few moments, their faces drawn and colorless. Dad was the first to rise. When we left the room that day I was between my parents, holding hands with both of them.

SPINNING IN CIRCLES

Kindergarten through second grade was a fun time, but not without a few bumps and bruises along the way. During that time Dad fell in love and got married. But they soon divorced and Dad and I were on our own again.

The most significant and exciting news, from my perspective, was that Dad got back into the sport of sled dog racing. He bought twenty dogs and had another twenty given to him. He started a business, Oregon Trail of Dreams, taking paying customers on sled dog rides around Mount Bachelor. I spent all the time I could with him. I was happiest when I was riding on the sled or playing with the dogs. I loved the mountain and the snow, but most of all I loved the dogs.

When there were chores to be done I pitched in and helped any way I could: packing small buckets of water to fill the dogs' water pans, taking turns stirring the dog food, and even using my little plastic scoop shovel to clean up messes. And when we had puppies it became my job to care for them. I was their first human contact. As soon as I stepped inside their pen a throng of yapping, yelping, hyper puppies descended on me and in their excitement they jumped on me, scratched me, and pulled at my pant legs until they knocked me down. And once I was on the ground they were like a pack of playful wolves, licking me, nuzzling me, tickling me, nipping at me.

Dad taught me how to handle the puppies. Whenever I went into the puppy pen I took a little switch with me. Any puppy that jumped on me I swatted on the top of the head. Dad always said if you swat a dog on the behind he will look at his behind. But if you swat him on the head he will look at you. I never swatted a puppy to hurt him. I would never, could never, do that. I just tapped a misbehaving puppy to get his attention. It worked.

We kept the dogs at a friend's farm until Dad bought a place way out in the country, away from everything and everyone. We moved to forty acres in the middle of the Badlands of Central Oregon, a National Wilderness Study Area. It was twenty-three miles to Bend, twenty-eight miles to Prineville, and twenty-five miles to Redmond. We lived in a trailer with no running water and no electricity. The water was trucked in and pumped into a cistern. We ran a generator for power. But the most difficult adjustment for me was that I had to change schools.

I had been perfectly content at Bear Creek Elementary. But now, enrolled at Buckingham Elementary on the outskirts of Bend, I began the most difficult period of my life. Many of the students at Buckingham Elementary came from privileged families, and cliques developed by the third grade. I did not fit into any of their exclusive cliques.

The popular kids dressed in trendy designer clothes. I threw on whatever was clean, and it never mattered if it matched: green and purple, blue and red, pink and green. Besides, I wore clunky glasses with incredibly thick lenses. I was always squinting at people and things, trying to bring them into focus so that I could see. As a result I was ostracized and ridiculed. Sometimes it went beyond normal childish teasing and I was the center of a cruel and deviant form of entertainment. In the hallway between classes, boys ran up from behind, grabbed my arms, and spun me in circles. In an effort to try to keep from falling I lurched this way and that, like a gangly moose on an icy pond. They tossed their caustic laughter and insults in my direction. "What's the matter, stupid blind girl, can't you see?" or, "Four Eyes, look where you're going!"

After an attack I stumbled around, trying to gain my bearings, trying to figure out where I was and in exactly which direction I was facing. If I made a mistake and started back the way I had come from or, heaven forbid, staggered into something, the kids whooped and hollered like this was the most hilarious thing they had ever witnessed. And as their laughter and jeering washed over me I felt like crawling into a hole and dying.

There was another visually impaired girl at Buckingham Elementary. Her name was Stacy. She had an additional strike against her because she was also an albino. Stacy suffered the same type of treatment I did; but when the boys spun her, she fought back like an enraged badger, screaming, shouting, and cursing until a teacher came on the run to see what the crisis was about. I was timid and passive, suffering in silence and allowing myself to be dominated by these hooligans who took such a perverse glee in exploiting my weaknesses.

Dad never knew what was happening at school, because I did not want to be a snitch and tell him. And so the struggle to survive continued until one day Dad happened to see a neighbor boy, Jimmy, walking along the road. Dad pulled over. "Hey, Jimmy, need a ride home?"

"Sure."

Jimmy climbed into the pickup and Dad, making small talk, inquired, "How's school going?"

"Fine."

"Been staying out of trouble?"

"I didn't do anything."

Jimmy's reply was so quick and defensive Dad knew something was eating at his conscience. Dad turned his head and saw that a tide of emotions was welling up behind Jimmy's eyes. "I was just joking. What's wrong?"

Jimmy blurted out, "I just feel real bad about what's happening at school with Rachael."

Dad's demeanor was very calm, but inside he was seething. "What's happening to Rachael?"

And that was when Jimmy broke down and started crying and all the ugly things that were happening poured out into the open, "There's this group of fifth-grade boys and every time they catch Rachael alone in the hall they pick on her."

Dad pulled off to the shoulder of the road and stopped. "Really? So what are they doing? How do they pick on her?"

Tears were spilling down Jimmy's cheeks. "They run up behind her in the hall, grab her by the arms, and spin her in circles. If she falls down, or stumbles into something, it's a big joke. And they call her names, too. They tease her all the time."

"Really?"

Jimmy whimpered. "I've wanted to tell someone for the longest time. I'm really sorry, Mr. Scdoris."

I was unaware that Dad knew about my personal problems until he asked me, "What's going on at school?"

"Nothing. Everything's fine."

"What's happening in the hallway? Tell me about the fifth-grade boys."

At that point I knew that he knew, but I tried to make light of it. "They're just playing. They're having fun. It just happens to be at my expense."

"I'm taking you to school tomorrow and we're going to sit down and talk to the principal. We're getting to the bottom of this and I guarantee you this crap won't be happening again. Not to you, not to anyone else."

"No, Dad. Don't say anything. You'll only make it worse." I argued with him, but secretly I was glad that the boys' outlandish behavior had been exposed. I hoped, I had secretly prayed, that something might be done about it. But I was also scared, scared of what the boys might do to me in retaliation. I could not sleep that night. I was that fearful.

The following morning Dad was on a mission. He marched me into the principal's office, informed the principal what was going on, and very forcefully stated, "Either you monitor the halls and make them safe for my daughter or I promise you that I will be here to monitor the halls myself. It's up to you."

"I had no idea such a thing was going on. You can be assured we will take care of the situation," the principal said.

I was excused to attend my first-period class, but midway through it I was called to the principal's office. The special education teacher was there, and so was Stacy. Stacy had already described the injustices we had been subjected to and I confirmed that what she said was true, as well as adding that the trouble was not confined to the hallway. "Some boys give me a hard time at recess. They run around and scream in my face and pull my hair. They're just boys being stupid. That's the way boys are."

The special education teacher wanted to know, "Can you tell me who's doing this? Can you give me names?"

Stacy and I never saw faces. Perhaps we could have identified exactly who was terrorizing us in the hallways and on the playground, but even if we knew for a certainty I do not know that we would have named names. At that point both of us felt pretty much scared to death.

The principal made a solemn promise to have the staff monitor the situation. But as far as I could tell, nothing really changed. Each evening when Dad asked if there had been any problems, I would lie and tell him no, that everything was hunky-dory.

NEW BEGINNINGS

Background Information

Rachael continued to be teased at school, so she transferred in the fifth grade to a new school, where she made a good friend. She lived with her mother and spent weekends and vacations with her father. Rachael began to think about becoming an Iditarod racer.

During the week I went through the motions of going to school and turning in my assignments. I lived for the weekends. Then I could spend time with my dogs. They were the most important things in my life. They were always happy to see me. They were my boys and girls. They loved me and I loved them back.

Any chance of my ever being able to compete in the Iditarod was a million miles away, especially considering that Dad refused to allow me to run the dogs. I pleaded with him to give me the opportunity to take them out on my own.

"Dad, do you think I do a lot of work around here?"

"Sure. And I appreciate it," he would say.

"Then when can I drive a team alone?"

I tried being rational: "Dad, I can't learn to drive a team any younger than I am right now, so why not let me do it today?"

"Someday, maybe."

Finally I resorted to indiscreet begging: "Dad, just let me drive the dogs. Please, please, pretty please."

I tried affection: "I love you, Dad. Will you please let me take out a team?"

"No!"

And yet, little by little, I thought I detected tiny chinks beginning to form in his resolve, in his tough exterior. Sometimes he actually talked to me. We progressed from a flat "No!" to a three-word response: "I said no!" From there we evolved to full-fledged, back-to-back sentences: "Honey, stop asking all the time. Someday I'll let you drive the dogs, but not today."

Spotting a moment of weakness, I would close in for the kill: "Can I drive them tomorrow? Can I, Daddy?" But it looked like tomorrow, or someday, would never arrive.

Dave Sims worked for Dad. Dave was more than just an employee; he was also a close personal friend. Lots of times I went on rides with him either on a tandem sled or as a passenger. Since I was unsuccessful in swaying Dad, I set my sights on Dave and began pestering him. If I convinced him I was capable of driving a dog team, maybe he would put in a good word for me.

But with the passing of time I came to believe that I would never be allowed the opportunity to drive a team of dogs, that I would never be given the chance to be on my own, that I would never run the Iditarod.

All my life, my entire life, someone had always been with me. Either I was in the company of an adult or I was operating under the buddy system with a responsible friend at my side. In school I was surrounded by other kids, and on the playground I was under constant supervision. I had never gone for a walk by myself, had never run on a trail through the woods without a companion. Not once had I been given the freedom of being alone, really alone.

One Saturday in mid-December it snowed a good six inches on the mountain. The trails were slow and the dogs, after working all day, had lost their nervous energy and were settled down. A member of the ski patrol stopped to visit for a moment and Dad asked him to make a pass on his snow machine and pack the Kids' Trail, a little one-mile loop that circled through the woods. I figured Dad was thinking that we might get a family who had grown tired of skiing and wanted a short sled dog ride before heading down the mountain. What I did not know was Dad had whispered to Dave, "This might be a good time to let Rachael make a run."

"Not a bad idea," Dave responded.

"She's eleven years old; think she's ready?" Dad asked.

"Ready as she'll ever be."

Dad and Dave hooked two of our best dogs, Coyote and Shane, to a sled. Both were leaders. Both had run the Iditarod. Coyote was an Alaskan husky, strong, dependable, and levelheaded. Shane had led a team that won the Yukon Quest. He was one of Dad's favorites and possibly the best dog Dad ever owned.

"Hey, Rachael," Dad called to me. "Do you want to make a run?"

"Sure," I said. I was always up for a run. I walked over to where Dave was holding the team, paused to pet Coyote and Shane before proceeding to the sled where Dad waited. "Who's going with me?"

"Just you," Dad said.

It took a second for that to sink in. And when it did, I assumed I had not heard him correctly. When I asked, "Just me?" my voice was more timid than I wanted it to be.

"Just you."

I moved quickly, before Dad could change his mind. My feet found the runners and my fingers gripped the handlebars. Dave stepped away. I spoke to the dogs: "Coyote, Shane. Hike!"

Instinct took over. From having run the tandem sled so many times I knew exactly what to do. But this was an entirely new sensation, to be alone, with only the dogs out in front. It was the coolest feeling. Fantastic. Exhilarating. I could use a thousand other adjectives and never begin to do justice to the incredible joy I felt at that moment. It was the thrill of a lifetime.

The start of the one-mile Kids' Trail is a fairly steep incline. I had been over it hundreds of times, but always in the basket or riding a tandem sled. It was an entirely new phenomenon to be doing it on my own. The shift of the runners beneath my feet was unlike any time before. The dogs ran faster. In fact, it was a little scary.

"The brake!" I could hear Dad's voice drifting to me from a long distance away. I knew he wanted me to slow down, but, quite the contrary, I wanted to go faster. I wanted the wind in my hair and the ice crystals kicked up by the dogs stinging my face. I wanted to race these dogs into the woods and never come back. I was intoxicated with this strange power of freedom, of being in command of so much raw energy, of being on my own. What did it matter that only

No End in Sight

two old dogs comprised my team, that we were on the Kids' Trail, that six inches of new snow was slowing the sled? The true significance of the moment was that finally I was taking my first step toward realizing my ultimate dream: to someday run the Iditarod. From inside me a noise began to emanate, bursting forth in an invigorating shout that caused me to throw back my head: "Wahoo!" It was a spontaneous thing, uttered in a moment of total exhilaration. Even I was surprised by it.

The trail dropped off the hill and we raced across an open flat. I rode the runners like a veteran musher as we careened into the first corner, and when we started the uphill climb I crossed over to one runner and used my free leg to pump, pushing to save my dogs and increase the sled's speed.

And just that quickly the mile run was over. We were back at the staging area and Dave was taking hold of Shane by the collar. We had barely come to a stop when I piled off the runners and sprinted to my dogs. I loved my two boys to death, threw my arms around their necks, hugged them, and showered them with kisses. I had never been so happy. I lavished every ounce of my affection on Shane and Coyote. They had taken me out and brought me back safely. One mile. The significance of that single mile was that if I could run one mile, it opened the possibility that I could run twelve hundred miles. The Iditarod had never been as close to a reality as it was at that moment.

THE RACE

Background Information

Rachael received an Iditarod sled as a gift. To get in shape to become a musher, she ran cross-country and track. She graduated from high school and began training for the Iditarod. At age twenty, she was ready for the Iditarod and went to Alaska. Paul Ellering would be her visual guide for the race. Among the people who went to Alaska to cheer her on were her father and Libby Riddles, the first woman to win the Iditarod. Rachael drew the tenth starting position for the Iditarod.

We spent the night at John and Mari Wood's place, but when it came time to go to bed I was full of nervous energy, and it took a long time for me to fall asleep. In the morning I indulged in a long, hot—very hot—shower. I knew it would be nearly a week until we reached the checkpoint at Takotna, where I would have the chance for another shower.

Because of the lack of snow at Wasilla, the traditional starting point, the restart of the Iditarod Trail Sled Dog Race was moved thirty miles to Willow Lake. We were directed onto the lake ice to the stake with my number 10 where we got busy dropping dogs. When they were fed and watered we took my racing sled down from the trailer. Dave Sims built it for me and promised it was "bulletproof" and would withstand anything the Iditarod could throw at it. I started sorting through the gear I was taking. The rules require mushers to carry all the equipment necessary for a musher and his dogs to survive under severe winter conditions.

A sled always steers best with the weight low and toward the back. From the many times I had practiced this procedure I knew where everything was supposed to go, and I started packing my red sled bag mounted to the sled. The heavy cooler full of dog food went at the bottom, in the back. The cooker to heat water, the dog pans, and the dipper for ladling dog food are light so I put those items near the front. My big Arctic sleeping bag followed by gloves, mittens, snacks, headlamps, goggles, sunglasses, and face shields—a necessity if the weather turned so cold that no skin could be exposed without suffering frostbite—were stowed, as were packages of dog food and dog treats. Lots of dog treats—salmon, hot dogs, and beef fat. I tied the ax in its leather sheath where I could reach it easily and made sure all other essential items were packed: dog booties, dog medicine and foot goop, spare lines and harness, cables for tying dropped dogs, tools for sled repair, a camera, CD player, CDs of some of my favorite music, and extra batteries. I puttered, taking my time, doing one thing and then stopping to be interviewed by the media or to give my dogs a love.

Mark Nordman, Iditarod race marshal, had requested that Paul and I give up the positions we drew and start at the back of the pack to avoid complications and criticism. There are a number of disadvantages for a musher in last place. The trail is horrible, torn up by all the traffic, dog teams, sleds, and snow machines. And, since every other team already passed that way, if any dog in front is sick with a stomach bug or virus there is a good chance the last team will pick up the germs and become sick later in the race. And even though I could not leave until the other seventy-eight mushers had departed, my time would begin when the number 10 musher was scheduled to depart: I would lose more than two hours before I ever left the starting line.

Everything I needed to do could have been done in an hour. But with six hours to kill, I puttered. I stretched and massaged the dogs, greased their feet and put booties on them. I checked out the wireless radio headsets that the K-9 unit of the Anchorage Police Department had loaned us. Having a wireless system, with a button Paul and I could keep inside our gloves, was certainly going to be an advantage over shouting. Members of the media stopped by for interviews, friends came to wish me well. I waited for my turn to go to the starting line.

I was surprisingly calm but could still feel the nervous tickle in the pit of my stomach, the way I used to feel before a big race in track. I think I was generally relaxed, though, because I knew I had done everything possible to prepare myself and my dogs. We were as ready as we were ever going to be.

The loudspeaker announced that Tyrell Seavey was the next musher to go and that he was one of five Seaveys to compete in the Iditarod. I ran to the chute, arriving as he was pulling to the starting line. I wished him well and on a whim gave him a good-luck kiss on the cheek. And then I stepped out of the way and he was off. I knew he had a good team and would be among the front-runners. The next time I would see him would be in Nome.

WILLOW TO YENTNA—45 MILES

One by one the mushers near us began to leave, and as each departed my dogs got more restless and eager to run. I did not want them waiting too long in harness expending useless energy in their excitement, and I delayed until the last minute before giving the go-ahead to have my team harnessed and hooked to the gangline. From that point forward everything in my world became a blur of motion and activity. Paul and his crew were just as busy.

Paul pulled forward, and my dogs, knowing they would soon get their chance to run, were wild in their excitement. My handlers did a fine job, petting the dogs and trying to keep them distracted. We pulled into the chute, and Paul sprinted toward me. He threw his arms around me in a quick embrace, reassured me we would reach Nome, ran back to his sled, hopped on the runners, and away he went. I moved forward until the brushbow of my sled was poised under the Iditarod banner. In front of me was a long chute lined with people, and beyond was the trail leading off into the unknown. I said a quick prayer, asking God to please take care of my dogs and me, and then I asked Him for one specific favor, "Please, God, don't let me crash on the first corner."

The handlers stepped away. The countdown happened quickly. I barely had time to hug Dad and clasp hands with Libby. She shouted over the roar of the crowd, "Show 'em what you can do, girl."

And then we were under way and the crowd, held back by a banner-lined snow fence, cheered as my sixteen racing huskies charged ahead, powering into the big sweeping right-handed corner. Paul was somewhere out in front. I could not see him. As we circled the frozen lake we began to close the gap, and I caught him at the point the trail turned off the lake ice and led up onto the first rolling hill.

We topped the ridge and the commotion so familiar in my world fell away. Ahead was eleven hundred miles of wilderness. I was ecstatic to leave behind the media, the crush of people, the noise, the confusion, and the schedule of scripted activities. From now on my world would be simple and basic. It would be about the dogs and our race to Nome. I let out a huge sigh of relief.

A group of people gathered around a campfire yahooed, and I realized I was far from alone. We passed other groups along the trail, and friendly voices called my name and wished me well. As we were going up a steep hill a woman ran over and handed me a necklace, telling me they were good-luck beads.

No End in Sight

"How are you doing?" Paul's voice spoke over my radio.

I depressed the finger button. "Couldn't be better."

The Outdoor Life Network helicopter hovered overhead, following every twist and turn as my dogs snaked through the trees and up and over the hills. The sun dropped into a bank of clouds, and the helicopter departed. As the light faded and darkness crept over the land, I thought that now, finally, I would be alone in the night, but we dropped down on the flat plain of the frozen Susitna River and every mile or so snow machines would be pulled into a circle like covered wagons, where bonfires would be roaring, and people would be partying and having a good time. Paul and I were running with headlamps, and as soon as the revelers saw us coming they would shout encouragement at us, and as we swept past they called out, asking if anyone was behind us. When we let them know we were the last two racers, they whooped and hollered some more and went back to their party.

This social scene lasted all the way to the checkpoint at Yentna. As we arrived, a host of other teams were resting beside the trail. We were directed to an open area, and Paul and I pulled in side by side. The soft snow made it difficult to set a snow hook to stake out the team. So I used my ax as an anchor, and to keep it from pulling out I set a bale of straw over the line. I took care of my dogs and tried to curl up on the straw and sleep with them, but I was still too excited to sleep. I walked inside a building where a nice woman said she was rooting for me and insisted I eat a plate of spaghetti. I did not have much of an appetite.

"Take my bed," she offered.

"Thank you, but I can't do that." I explained, "I'm not allowed to have anything special. If you offer your bed to me you have to offer it to every other musher."

I found a place to sleep under a table and curled up there, but woke up when the woman placed a sheet over me. Then a man woke me because he was leaving and needed his stuff sack that I had been using as a pillow. Other people stepped over me and on me. I finally gave up and went out into the night, looked after my dogs, and got ready to hit the trail.

YENTNA TO SKWENTNA—34 MILES

We left Yentna in the dark and ran all night with headlamps. Once in a while Paul called to me on the radio or I caught a glimpse of his headlamp, but mostly it was wonderful to feel alone in the big Alaskan night. The trail was rough, chewed up by mushers in front of us riding their brakes on the downhill stretches and leaving deep furrows. But my dogs took the winding trail smoothly. I passed some teams and moved up to 65th place. If everything went according to plan, I thought I had a chance to finish in the middle of the pack. That would be almost like a victory. But deep inside I knew my thinking at this early point of the race was rash, and that on the Iditarod trail good things and bad things had a way of happening when you least expected them.

When the sun came up, harsh light fell on the white peaks of the Alaska Range, looming ahead of us like an impenetrable barrier. Two of my dogs tangled, and I stopped to fix the problem. Lisa's right hind leg was caught in her tugline, but it appeared to be a rope burn, nothing more. When we arrived at the Skwentna checkpoint I treated the rope burn with Algyval—an anti-inflammatory medication—rubbed some antibiotic ointment on it, and gave the leg a massage. The injury was not swollen, and she did not favor the leg.

Paul and I had planned a conservative race. Our schedule called for a six-hour layover in Skwentna. After the dogs were fed, Paul and I grabbed a bite to eat. Paul told me the vets wanted him to drop Cletus. He was one of the dogs I had given to Paul for the race to make our teams equal. In the Tustumena I had had to drop Cletus because of an inflammation in the tendon in his left leg. But it had seemed fine in our training leading up to the Iditarod.

"Is it his tendon?" I asked.

"No. He has a respiratory problem," Paul said.

As a pup Cletus had gotten dust in his lungs, and every once in a while, if the temperature was warm and he was working hard, he had an occasional problem with coughing. I did not think the condition would bother him in Alaska, but the weather was unseasonably warm, hovering around or slightly above the freezing mark.

The veterinarian crew took Cletus to the landing strip to fly him back to Anchorage, where Dad would pick him up and care for him. A half hour later a man on a snow machine roared up and said, "Your dog got loose and they can't catch him. Jump on the sled and I'll run you out there. Maybe he'll come to you."

I got on the sled attached to the snow machine, and the driver roared off. I held on with both hands and tried not to get bounced out. When we reached the makeshift airstrip I asked a fellow leaning against a plane, "Did they catch the dog?"

He shrugged. "Don't guess so."

"Do you know where he is?"

He seemed totally disinterested. "He went running off. A couple of the vets chased after him."

No End in Sight

I thought, *Oh, that's great because Cletus is afraid of his own shadow.* I knew that nobody was going to be able to chase down a sled dog on foot. "What direction were they headed?"

"Don't know. Wasn't paying no attention."

The man on the snow machine took me through the woods until we found two men chasing a dog. I got off and called Cletus. He immediately came to me. I put Cletus on the sled, and we rode back to the airstrip, where I loaded Cletus onto the plane.

After that the fellow on the snow machine asked me a series of questions about what I could or could not see, how the race was going, and if I had any reservations about the upcoming trail through the Alaska Range. Finally I told him, "I'm running a race. I've got to get back to my team."

As it turned out, the fellow on the snow machine was Craig Medred, outdoor editor of the *Anchorage Daily News.* He had written a number of critical stories about me and my quest to run the Iditarod. He once referred to me as "an eighteen-year-old musher pushed into the race by her boosterish father," and declared there was no way I could ever drive my dog team over the Alaska Range. In his latest story he would point out that I had enough visual ability to catch my dog after it got loose, leash it, and walk around a Cessna 185 without bumping into the propeller or the strut beneath the wing. He added, "But when she returned to checkpoint headquarters, after having been there once before, she mistook the cabin of Joe and Norma Delia for the checkpoint cabin. Although the buildings have some similarities, they are quite different and located in distinct settings."

If I ever run into Mr. Medred again I will ask him why he did not feel an obligation, or have the common courtesy, to introduce himself to me before he interviewed me, and I suppose I should apologize for having too much sight for a blind person.

Background Information

Rachael continued racing, having passed her first test—Happy River Steps—a steep, nearly vertical drop down a hill. Rachael stopped at various checkpoints along the race. She learned that other racers had scratched—or dropped out of the race. Some of her dogs became sick, her sled crashed, and she hurt her hand. Later, the gangline sliced the tip of her middle finger. Reporter Peter Jennings from *ABC News* interviewed Rachael and named her Person of the Week.

Ophir had been the center of a placer mining region, but only a handful of miners remained to actively work the old claims. Other than a few buildings, very little was left to indicate this village had ever been of any significance. We stayed at Ophir for only three hours and then set out on one of the longest—and loneliest—runs of the entire race. The sun was up and already the temperature was above freezing.

A few miles west of Ophir the Iditarod Trail separates into the northern and southern routes. On odd years the route takes the southern loop and on even years the mushers swing north. This is done to accommodate the villages along the Yukon who asked to be included on the Iditarod Trail. We swung south and began the long run to Iditarod in the heat of the day, slicing through a forest of spruce and birch. Snow machines and other mushers had beaten the trail into a deep quagmire that made for slow going. After ten miles the country opened onto a broad tundra plain and the wind picked up and blew in our faces.

A competitive musher will run his dogs in a rhythm of six to eight hours and rest six to eight hours. After the long layover at Takotna we thought the dogs would be rested and rejuvenated, but the combination of a bad trail, warm temperatures, and diarrhea had robbed them of strength. To compound matters wet snow began sticking to the runners and the burden became even heavier for the dogs to pull. Traveling slow, like we were, takes all the fun out of a race, and monotony and boredom began to pull me down. I could feel my energy seeping away, replaced by discouragement and depression. Dogs can totally read a human. If I ever allowed my rising frustration to become obvious to the dogs, they would pick up on it in a heartbeat. Anyone who has ever had a dog for a pet knows how it reacts to an owner's bad mood or a harsh word.

"You're a great bunch of dogs," I lied. "You're running so well," I lied some more. "Keep going. Good boy, Jovi. Way to go, Mandy. Angel, you look fabulous."

My dogs run to please me and because it is fun for them. They are bred to run, but when running becomes a struggle they lose interest in a hurry. To motivate them I stopped often, gave them loves, and tried to pump a little enthusiasm back into their tired bodies. I let them know that, much like a long-distance runner on the track, they could push through this pain, and once they had their second wind everything would be better. I was animated and expressive in my gestures and with my words. I switched leaders often so unnecessary stress was not put on any one or two dogs. We were a team, and as a team we would get through this trying stretch of trail together. I handed out salmon treats, hot dogs, and beef fat.

No End in Sight

Tyrell had warned me about the long run from Ophir to Iditarod. He said it could prove an unpleasant experience for my dogs. However, once they made it through that stretch, they would gain confidence and begin to believe in themselves. He had said a few doubts might even creep into my thinking, and I might have concerns about whether my team was strong enough, physically and mentally, to reach the finish line.

We were hoping to reach a cabin that is used by travelers on the Iditarod trail called Don's Cabin, but due to the heat we were forced to take a long break. We rested five hours, then the sun went down, cooler air moved in, and we were able to get back on the trail. After Don's Cabin the miles slowly passed under the runners, and I told myself that even though we were moving slowly, at least we were moving.

In the darkness Paul called back, "Ice bridge! Open water ahead!"

Paul was having trouble coaxing his dogs over the ice bridge that extended only partway over a stream, leaving a gap of several feet. After a moment's hesitation his lead dogs leaped the opening, and the other dogs had no choice but to follow, pulling the sled, and Paul, across to the far side. And then it was my turn.

Something told me to switch leaders and put Eyes up front. She was not afraid of open water. But we had spent so much time on the trail I decided the leaders I had could handle it. But Jovi, one of my leaders, was afraid of open water and refused to jump across the span. I ventured out onto the ice bridge and picked up Jovi to toss him across. The ice bridge began to sink beneath me.

"Toss me a line," called Paul.

I sloshed my way back to my sled, pulled out a line, tied off to Jovi's neckline, and tossed Paul the other end. Again I returned to my sled, stepped on the runners, pulled the snow hook, and went for it. With Paul pulling on the line the dogs made it to the opposite side. When the sled reached the ice bridge it collapsed, my feet came off the runners, and I was dunked in the icy water. The only part of me that did not get drenched was the top of my head.

If this had been a typical winter, with temperatures twenty or thirty degrees below zero, this could have been a critical situation and we would have had to stop to build a fire so I could warm up and dry out. But again, if this had been a typical winter the ice bridge would have held.

I shrugged off several layers of clothes and stripped the liners from my boots, dumping out the water and putting in new liners that were soaked within a few minutes. Then we kept moving. I was a little concerned about hypothermia, but I was never cold, thanks to that warm wind and polypropylene, Polarfleece, and

Gore-Tex that wicked away most of the moisture from my body. The wind dried me from the outside in, but my feet remained wet and uncomfortable and made squishing sounds every time I shifted my weight.

The steady rhythm of the dogs' feet padding along the trail hypnotized me. Or it might have been the chill of being dunked in the icy stream. Or the fatigue factor might have been setting in. At any rate that night I became very, very sleepy. I began to drift off for a moment or two with my eyes wide open, and sometimes with my eyes closed. I would awaken, and my body would be draped over the handlebar.

The moon played peekaboo behind the clouds. Even in the darkness, with just the tunnel of light from the headlamp, I could sense the open country becoming more confining, with willows and brush crowding both sides of the trail. And then I began to hallucinate. I saw people standing beside the trail, never anyone I recognized. They talked and laughed among themselves like they were waiting for my arrival at a nonexistent checkpoint. I turned and as the light of my headlamp swept over them they stopped talking and turned their heads to stare at me as we passed. Sometimes they were back from the trail and I only heard voices, catching snippets of conversations, never any intelligible words, but I assumed they were talking about me, or my team.

Even though my rational mind told me these people did not exist, it was strange and perplexing and incredibly spooky to deal with. I tried to drink some water and managed to choke down a Reese's peanut butter cup and a handful of trail mix. I had difficulty swallowing.

We came to a series of small hills. To set a good example for my dogs I ran every upgrade. On the downhills I rode the runners. Dawn was beginning to color the eastern sky and all I wanted was sleep. Eventually I got my wish and when I awoke, slumped over the back of my sled, I saw my dogs curled up in the snow. I had no concept of how much time had passed. Paul came back to see where I was and we decided, since my dogs were already settled in and not inclined to move, that we would rest. I shared some Gummi Bears with Paul and we both grabbed short naps.

When we pushed on we discovered the settlement of Iditarod was only a couple miles from where we had camped. The town of Iditarod, all I saw, consisted of two old cabins, a new mushers' cabin, and an outhouse. Inside the mushers' cabin was a diesel stove, cranked up and hot. The warm air hit me like a punch in the stomach. A screen was suspended above the stove where mushers had laid gear to dry. I got out of my clothes, pulled on a pair of dry long underwear, and hung everything that was damp by the stove to dry.

Mushers, volunteers, and race officials were milling around and talking. All the commotion made my head spin. The heat made me drowsy. Everyone was so nice and asked questions about my experiences. I tried to formulate answers, but my mind was numb, as though it were still out somewhere on the trail and had not quite caught up with the rest of me. After feeding my dogs a hot meal and tending to personal matters, I climbed up into the loft in the cabin and slept six straight hours.

When we were ready to leave I dropped Karelan. He had not been contributing to the team. Mostly he just goofed off and ran with a slack tugline, letting the other dogs do the work. He had become a liability.

We had reached the halfway point in the race. I remembered someone telling me if I made it past the first three days on the Iditarod the going would get easier because the dogs and I would become hardened to the trail. Others said that at the halfway point the trail became easier mentally because you knew you had the toughest half under your belt and that in another six days or so it would all be over. I was not so sure.

IDITAROD TO SHAGELUK—65 MILES

We followed the Iditarod River for a few miles and then entered a succession of rolling hills that lay like random furrows. The trail followed a maddening course up and over these hills. Logically it would seem the best route was between ridges, but most often we had to summit the tall hills and drop down the far side. The wind blew constantly in our faces, and the trail was lousy. The crust had been broken apart by snow machines spinning their tracks going uphill, and on the downhills mushers had ridden their brakes and dug deep gullies.

On the uphills I ran or pumped. It was something like trying to run in a bowl of sugar. At the brow of the hills I was able to catch my breath for a minute or two, riding the brake to keep from running over my dogs. I was working hard, taking frequent sips of water, and scrounging in my pockets for some tidbit to snack on. I ate Gummi Bears, candy, and jerky.

Just when it seemed the hills would continue forever, the trail mercifully began a long, slow descent into a valley cut by the Innoko and Yukon Rivers. When we reached the river ice I heard the distant barking of dogs, and in a few more miles caught the whiff of wood smoke. Both were sure signs we were nearing civilization, or at least the village of Shageluk.

We pulled into the checkpoint at Shageluk, and I frantically searched for my bootie bag, which also included the coats for my dogs. It was not tied on the sled in its usual place. I had lost it on the trail somewhere. I tried to remember when I had seen it last and concluded it had to have been where we dropped out of the hills toward the valley floor.

"I'll run back and check the trail," offered one of the volunteers. "Don't worry. I'll find it." He jumped on his snow machine and departed up the trail with a rooster tail of snow blowing up behind him and the loud whine of his powerful engine.

But I was worried. If I did not have that bag, then my dogs would not have booties to protect their feet. They had to have booties. And we needed the jackets, too, because if the temperature dropped—and it was almost certain to drop as we approached the Yukon River—my dogs would be cold and would burn precious calories staying warm. They needed to save every calorie for the race. I was sick with worry and I blamed myself. I was the one who had lost the bag. I was a terrible person. I should have been more alert. Dang it.

After feeding my dogs I made my way to where we were supposed to sleep. It was a round building, and for some peculiar reason the roundness bothered me so I hiked to the headquarters building and lay on the floor. I still could not sleep because I was too stressed out about losing the bootie bag. A Native woman said she was fixing moose stew and cooking salmon and would let me know when it was ready to eat.

I must have dozed because several kids shook me awake, "Rachael, wake up. Wake up. Dinner is ready, Rachael."

I was so tired I just wanted to lie on the floor and sleep, but I knew the woman had worked hard to fix this special meal so I forced myself to get up and eat. The food was delicious. Afterward I was able to make a call to Mom and then I tried to sleep, but instead of sleeping I started crying because my dogs were sick and skinny and I had lost the bootie bag. I was an emotional baby. I could not seem to snap myself out of it and cried myself to sleep.

"Rachael, I've got your bootie bag," said the man who had ridden up the trail on the snow machine and who now appeared before me. "Sandy McKee found it and picked it up. She gave it to me. Here it is."

I was so grateful that I jumped up, thanked him profusely, and gave him a kiss on the cheek. I lay back down and it was as though a thousand-pound weight had been lifted from me. My muscles went slack and I had the most relaxing sleep of my life. It was only a half hour, but it was all I needed.

No End in Sight

Background Information

Rachael continued racing, pushing toward the Yukon River. Her dogs were becoming increasingly tired and sick. Rachael hallucinated again. She had to drop two of her dogs from the race and was down to ten dogs.

GRAYLING TO EAGLE ISLAND—60 MILES

Ten solid dogs would be sufficient to finish the race. But I had ten sick dogs. And as we departed Grayling that night and returned to the Yukon River ice, I watched my dogs in the light from my headlamp, searching for the telltale signs that my dogs had had enough and wanted to call it quits. Some dogs will give their feelings away by the way they hang their heads, or their gait, or by the way they drop their tails, or even something as subtle as how they hold their ears. If a dog's ears flop down, it means the dog is unhappy and disheartened. Every dog is different. With a little encouragement some will respond, dig down, and find a hidden reserve; others will not. The ultimate job of every musher is to read the dogs and calculate exactly what they are capable of achieving.

The Yukon drains a huge area, all the interior of Alaska from the Brooks Range to the Alaska Range. Cold air, moving like water, courses along over the ice and the wind mimics the cold. A cold wind greeted us, blowing straight into our faces. I knew this was going to make it more difficult and was glad I had put coats on all the dogs.

Before we departed Grayling, Paul gave me one of his ski poles, and I used it to push off as we traveled. I worked the ski pole and helped the dogs, but several times fatigue overtook me and I caught myself napping. I would awaken but even in my sleep I continued to push with the pole. And then one time I awoke to find that the ski pole was gone. I had dropped it. There was no one behind me who could pick it up. I was the last musher in the race. If I managed to hold on, and finish the race, I would win the red lantern, the award given to the last team to reach Nome.

We ran through the long night. I pumped with one leg for a while and then the other, not only to help the dogs but also to help me stay awake. As morning dawned, my concern for my dogs and my own fatigue, as well as the blasting of the constant wind and the bleak whiteness of the landscape, merged to form a white blur. Occasionally, as we flat-tracked near one side of the river or came upon islands, I was aware of the deep green of spruce and the light-colored birch trees. My dogs never seemed to take notice. They kept to their languid pace. They were tired and sore and disheartened. I could sympathize with them. I had an assortment of aches and pain of my own. My face was windburned and my lips were chapped. My hip and finger still bothered me. The muscles in my forearms were sore from gripping the handlebars. I had scrapes, nicks, and cuts. When I pulled off my gloves my hands looked like working man's hands. And my feet were bruised and wet and cold. I was groggy, scatterbrained, and bushed. But I could deal with my discomforts. What bothered me was the deteriorating health of my dogs. I stopped often, dispensing treats and words of support and confidence.

The dogs finally decided they had had enough. They stopped and lay down on the ice, immediately curling up with their backs to the wind. There was nothing I could do except give them the break they demanded. I plopped myself down on the front of my sled. I figured to be there a minute or two but I fell asleep. Half an hour passed. I had foolishly not been wearing gloves nor did I tuck my hands into a protective pocket. When I awoke my fingers were cold and useless. If it had been really cold and I had made such a critical mistake, I could easily have lost my fingers.

I tucked my hands under my armpits to warm them enough to be functional. My dogs never moved, and I was not sure if we could continue. I was depressed and desperate, wanting something, anything, to go my way for a change.

It was then that Jay Rowan, my friend who had died in a tragic swimming accident, spoke to me. He was not a hallucination. I sensed his presence and he spoke to me, but not the way two people talk. His words simply formed in my mind.

"Rachael, the leaders are only three hundred miles ahead of you. You can do this. I know you're hurting. I know you're discouraged. But you're going to get back on that sled and you're going to pick off the stragglers ahead of you one by one. You're going to finish this race. Get going, girl."

Jay's words inspired me. I got up, pulled on my chore gloves, and got my dogs on their feet. I gave each a quick massage and some love. Paul doubled back and asked how I was doing. I told him we had taken a short break and we were about ready to go. When I called to my dogs they moved forward.

As we traveled I evaluated my dogs with a critical eye. Angel was the only dog in my team that seemed the least bit interested in leading and she was now my thinnest dog. She had the heart but not the physical stamina to continue. Bernard, Ned, and Dutchess were nearly as skinny. If I dropped all four at Eagle Island I would be down to six dogs and have no leaders. A dog team without at

No End in Sight

least one strong leader is not a dog team. Of my remaining dogs—Eyes, Possum, Jovi, Mandy, Brick, and Seth—none was capable of carrying the team.

I did some soul searching, trying to determine if I was strong enough mentally and physically to hold six dogs together. Cim Smyth had done it, running the last five hundred miles to Nome with only five dogs. And he had set the record for the fastest time from Safety to Nome. But I was not Cim Smyth. I was a rookie and I was fried. I had been holding this team together since Takotna and I was not sure how much longer I could pull off such a miracle.

I continued to pump, pushing off with my right leg ten or twenty times and then switching to my left. I would have a tough decision to make when we reached Eagle Island. I have always been told to never consider scratching going into a checkpoint; that you always take care of your dogs, eat and sleep, and then look at the world from a fresh perspective. I might decide, okay, maybe I could hold them together to Kaltag. And if we made it to Kaltag, then maybe we could limp into Unalakleet, and on to Shaktoolik, Koyuk, and Elim. If we made Elim, we would only be a hundred miles or so from Nome. A hundred miles—now that was definitely doable.

Breaking a race down like that is a distance runner's trick. In the middle of a 3000 you tell yourself, "Only five laps to go," and you count them down: 4, 3, 2, 1, and done. I played the same game in the Iditarod. Go one lap at a time, or as John Patten had drummed into my head, "Small bites are easier to swallow."

We reached Eagle Island checkpoint. It was nothing more than a single tent set up especially for the race in an endless sea of wilderness. I gave the dogs an absolute smorgasbord, and they turned their noses up at the lamb, chicken, and salmon and the hot dogs and beef fat, too. The only thing they were the least bit interested in was the Atta Boy kibbles. But they only nibbled at it. That was a bad sign.

It was obvious from the thinness of the dogs, but the veterinarian was trying to make conversation and asked if the diarrhea medicine had helped. I was honest. There was really no sense in trying to be deceitful. My team was in trouble.

"I haven't been able to keep weight on them, not since Takotna. That's where the diarrhea started getting bad and they began losing weight. Until now they've eaten pretty well, but it doesn't matter how much they eat, or how much fat I pump into them, it all goes straight through their systems. And now they don't have an appetite for anything, not even the treats."

I decided to take some time for myself. I had heard about Eagle Island, and the word from other mushers was that the wind always blew and the checkpoint was nothing more than a dismal tent with a little Coleman heater that never kicked out enough heat to warm the place. But that was in years past. I ducked through the canvas flap and found a palace in the form of a four-wall room made of plywood and a heater that could melt the polar ice cap. I had the heater to myself. I hung up my clothes and dropped a Ziploc bag with Becki's special taco soup into a pan of boiling water. It was one of the finest meals I had ever eaten. When Paul came in I told him he was going to enjoy his food. He soon confirmed my view, saying he had never eaten taco soup but that he was now an enthusiastic convert.

After that, with warm food in my belly and a cocoon of warm air surrounding me, I flopped down on one of the bunks and slept several hours. Jim Gallea, a musher I first met when he ran the Atta Boy 300, woke me. He had run three Iditarod races, but I remembered he was going to medical school at the University of Washington and would not participate this year. I was momentarily confused as to why he was there, but quickly grasped that he was an official.

"We need to talk," Jim told me. He said the veterinarian was of the opinion I should drop four of my dogs.

"But that will put me down to six."

"I know," Jim said, understanding my dilemma.

"Six dogs," I repeated. It did not seem fair. I had given Paul six of my best dogs, and five of them were still on his ten-dog team. If I had had those dogs . . . I stopped myself from thinking of what might have been and faced the fact that I was down to six dogs. I had no front end, no leaders. And several of the six were thin and sick. If I continued I would be putting a tremendous amount of pressure on those six dogs. In good conscience I could not do that to the dogs I loved. I had raised them from puppies, trained and watched them develop into the athletes they had become. It was not right for me to push them past the point where the race was no longer a fun experience.

I spoke with Mark Nordman—the Iditarod race marshal—on the satellite telephone, and he left it up to me, the decision to try to continue or to pull out of the race. It was my decision alone. If I pushed my dogs too far, I would have to live with the consequences of that. And if I pulled out, I would have to live with that, too.

I stepped outside to talk to my dogs and wrestled with my decision. When I saw my spent team and saw the way they were curled up on the straw, how skinny they had become from the diarrhea-causing virus, my decision was made for me. There was only one choice I could make.

I looked upward into the sodden sky. "I held them together as long as I could. My dogs are sick. If there was any way for us to go on, you know I would. I have to scratch. I'm sorry, Jay."

After I had made peace with Jay I went inside the tent, sat on a bunk, and cried. Paul came over and wrapped a beefy arm around me. He knew without my having to say the words. He felt bad for me. I told him, "You better get going. You can pass a few teams on the way in. Or you can stay where you are, in last place, and collect the red lantern." I tried to smile.

"I don't think so," he said. "It wouldn't be the same without you. Besides, I'm the kind of guy who believes in leaving with the same girl he brought to the dance."

I remembered something Dave Sims told me before I left Central Oregon. One day we were sitting on the couch talking about the Iditarod and he said, "If you go up there and you don't finish, then you *have* to do it again. If you finish, you *can* do it again, if you want to."

I said, "I just don't want anybody to make this a sight thing. Saying I pulled out because of my vision. This is a dog thing."

"Don't worry about that," Jim Gallea said. "Nobody doubts you. You proved what you could do. You passed all the tough places with flying colors. Anyone can scratch because their dogs got sick. Look at Rick Swenson and Charlie Boulding, two of the most famous men in our sport. They pulled out when their dogs got sick. It happens. You can come back next year and you'll get to Nome."

All that remained of my 2005 Iditarod run was to make it official. Jim got a piece of paper and a Sharpie. He wrote my name and the words "Scratched at Eagle Island." I signed it.

Then I called Dad on the satellite phone and told him. He said, "I'm sure you made the right decision. I'm proud of you, and, honey, I love you."

Epilogue

Rachael again raced the Iditarod in 2006, placing fifty-seventh out of eighty-three mushers. Her motto is "Always shoot for the moon, and even if you miss, you will land among the stars."

Beyond the Book

Adventure Alaska!

Beckham's Tundra Trips and Tours

Alaskan thrills by land, water, snow, or air

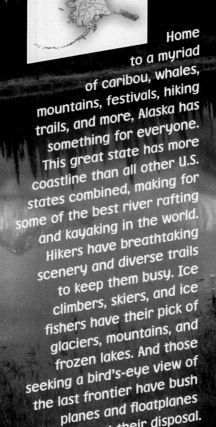

Home to a myriad of caribou, whales, mountains, festivals, hiking trails, and more, Alaska has something for everyone. This great state has more coastline than all other U.S. states combined, making for some of the best river rafting and kayaking in the world. Hikers have breathtaking scenery and diverse trails to keep them busy. Ice climbers, skiers, and ice fishers have their pick of glaciers, mountains, and frozen lakes. And those seeking a bird's-eye view of the last frontier have bush planes and floatplanes at their disposal.

ALASKAN GEOGRAPHY

Alaska is the largest state in the United States, at 586,412 square miles. Surrounded by ocean and filled with lakes, rivers, tundra, and forest—many of which are part of national refuges and reserves—Alaska is also home to volcanoes, islands, and marshlands.

BY LAND

Take one of our backpacking trips to Lake Clark National Park, where you'll discover icy river crossings, off-trail hiking, and glacier walks.

BY WATER

Enjoy sea kayaking in Resurrection Bay, river rafting on Six-Mile River, and canoeing among any of Alaska's winding rivers and streams.

BY SNOW

Those with a competitive edge might want to take a stab at the Iditarod sled-dog race in March. (This trip fills up fast!) Others can go snowshoeing across the tundra or ice skating under a midnight sun.

BY AIR

Experience a view like no other as you board a bush plane and visit tiny villages inaccessible by road. Or watch caribou herds from a hawk's view as you fly over sun-glazed glaciers.

Extension Activity

Connecting with a Character: Choose a minor character from *No End in Sight.* (a) Explain why you chose this character, and discuss two ways this person had an impact on the main character's life. (b) Think of someone who has had an impact in this way on your life. Describe this person and two ways this person has affected you. (c) Write a summary of your paper.

Paper Requirements: Paper must begin with a title page that lists the paper's title, your name, and the date. Paper must be two or three pages long (not including the title page).

Also By The Author

If you enjoyed *No End in Sight,* you may enjoy these other books by Rick Steber:
- *Cowboys* (nonfiction; Tales of the Wild West series)
- *Oregon Trail* (nonfiction; Tales of the Wild West series)
- *Pacific Coast* (nonfiction; Tales of the Wild West series)
- *Pioneers* (nonfiction; Tales of the Wild West series)
- *Women of the West* (nonfiction; Tales of the Wild West series)

Related Topics

If you enjoyed the topics discussed in *No End in Sight,* you may enjoy these other books that explore similar topics:
- *The Earliest Americans* by Helen Roney Sattler and Jean Day Zallinger (historical account of native civilizations, beginning with peoples who may have used a land bridge between Alaska and Siberia)
- *Gold Rush Dogs* by Claire Rudolf Murphy and Jane G. Haigh (nonfiction; celebration of notable dogs that took part in the Alaska-Yukon Gold Rush)
- *Gutsy Girls: Young Women Who Dare* by Tina Schwager and Michele Schuerger (nonfiction; stories about young women who have played extreme sports or performed challenging feats)
- *Race Across Alaska: First Woman to Win the Iditarod Tells Her Story* by Libby Riddles and Tim Jones (nonfiction; account of how Riddles became the first woman to win the Iditarod)
- *Winterdance: The Fine Madness of Running the Iditarod* by Gary Paulsen (nonfiction; narrative of Paulsen's Iditarod adventure)

TRIAL
—BY—
ICE

A Photobiography of Sir Ernest Shackleton

By K. M. Kostyal

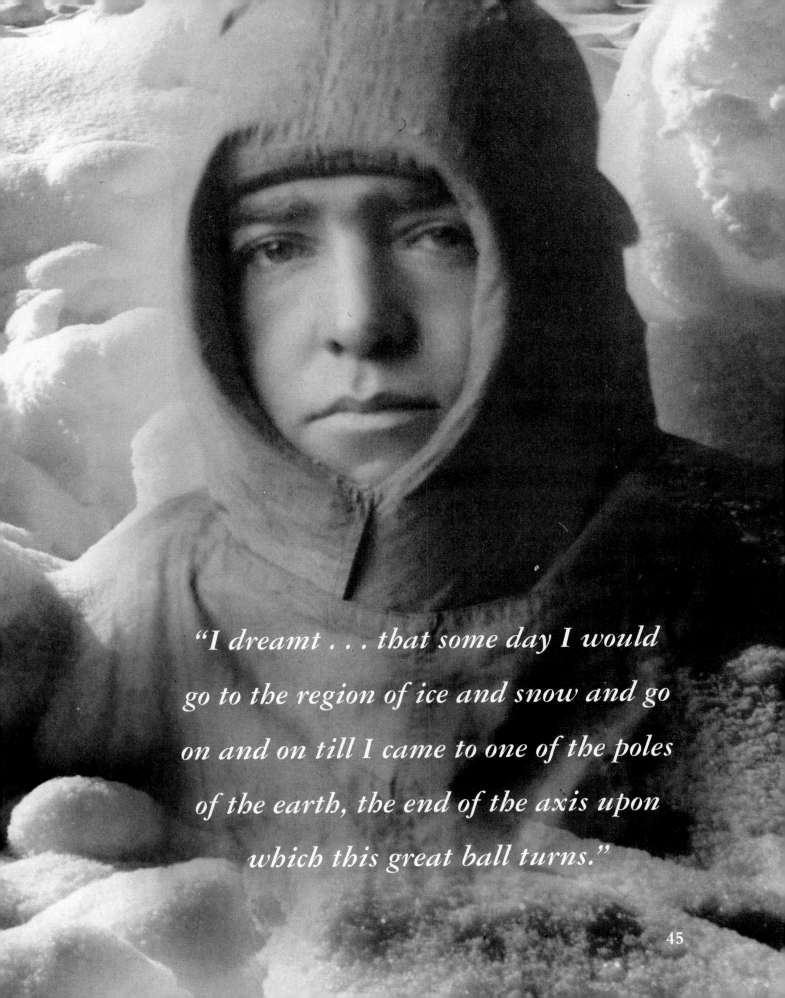

"I dreamt . . . that some day I would go to the region of ice and snow and go on and on till I came to one of the poles of the earth, the end of the axis upon which this great ball turns."

45

Ernest Shackleton towards the end of his life. He died in January of 1922.

FOREWORD

"Are you related to the Antarctic explorer Ernest Shackleton?" Since childhood, I have been asked that question. My father, Edward, was Ernest Shackleton's younger son, and I cannot remember a time when I was not aware of the part the great white continent had played in the life of my family.

Photographs from my grandfather's expeditions hung on the walls at home: beautiful black-and-white images from the early years of the century. They showed a world of snow and ice; bearded men in strange, shapeless garments; a little ship being slowly crushed in the ice, her decline more shocking in each photograph until she is finally only a skeleton of a ship. As a child, I was always particularly fascinated by one photograph. It showed the huskies (the sled dogs) sitting patiently on the ice beside the wreck of the ship that had been their home, her end not far away, their future in doubt.

Ernest Shackleton died at the start of his third expedition. He was only 47. My father was nine years old. He did not have the chance to know his father very well (explorers were away for years at a time then), yet he, too, became an explorer. At the age of 20 he went to Borneo and then to Ellesmere Island in the Canadian Arctic. He avoided the Antarctic because he did not want to seem to be trading on his father's name. When I was a little girl, I remember sitting on the coalhouse roof with my brother one day, pretending it was a ship. I made him promise that he, too, would explore, to make it three generations. And he did. He took part in an expedition to Devon Island, in the Canadian Arctic.

I did get to the Antarctic, nearly a hundred years after my grandfather, on a naval ship bearing the same name as his ship—*Endurance.* It was only a small glimpse of the Antarctic he had known, but it was an unforgettable experience. Perhaps after reading this excellent book, some of you too will be inspired to visit the great white south in the footsteps of Sir Ernest Shackleton.

Alexandra Shackleton

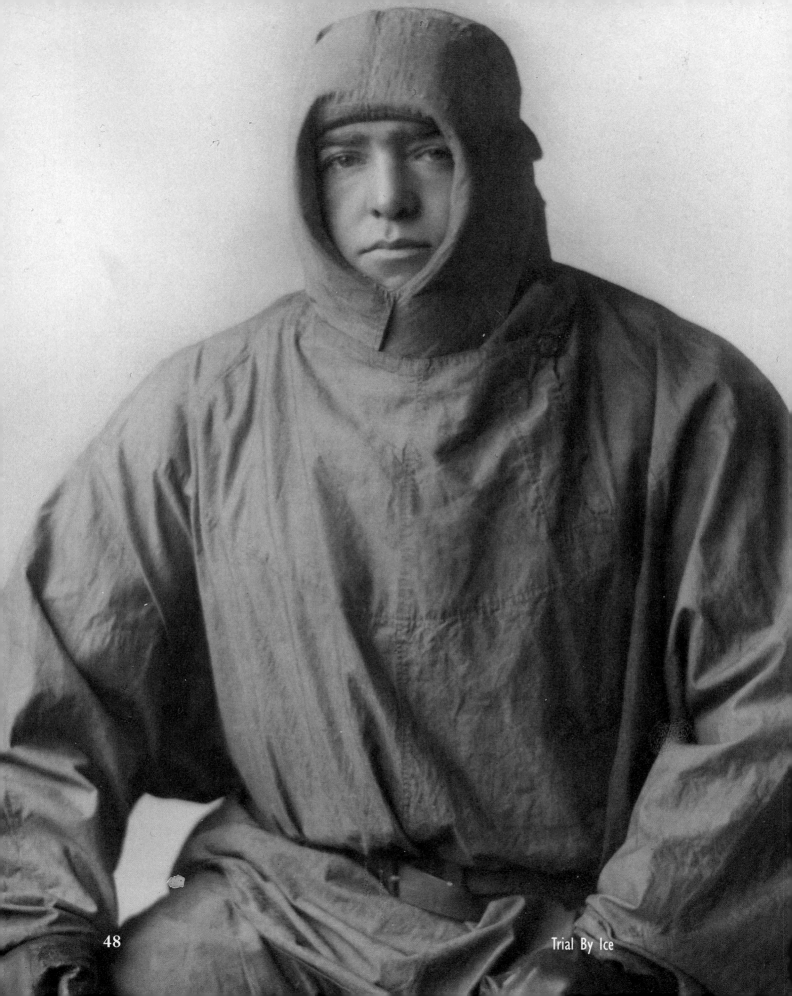

"The cliffs are of a dazzling whiteness, with wonderful blue shadows. Far inland higher slopes can be seen, appearing like dim blue or faint golden fleecy clouds."

The wild frozen beauty of Antarctica was a long way from the gentle green hills of Ireland's County Kildare, where Ernest Henry Shackleton was born. At his birth in 1874 no one could have imagined that this baby would grow up to be one of the world's greatest Antarctic explorers. In fact, it's doubtful that anyone in Ireland gave much thought to the southern continent at the end of the Earth.

The world of Ernest's early childhood was simple. People still traveled by horse and buggy, and there were no airplanes or telephones. An old castle topped a hill near the Shackleton family's rambling house, and country lanes crisscrossed the area's endless potato fields. But things were not good in Ireland. The potato crops were poor, and people suffered. When Ernest was six, his landowner father decided to begin a new life. He applied to study medicine at the university in Dublin, and the family left behind country life for the city.

Towering above his brother and eight sisters, Ernest stands at the center of a family portrait. Dressed for one of his early Antarctic expeditions (left), Shackleton wears his polar "helmet" and tunic.

After Ernest's father became a doctor, the family moved from Ireland to England and settled in a London suburb called Sydenham. Ernest, the older son in the big Shackleton family of two boys and eight girls, was good-natured and adored by his sisters. Even though school bored him and he was quick to join in a schoolyard brawl, Ernest loved to read, and he had a vivid imagination. He attended a secondary school

called Dulwich College where a publication later described him as a "rather odd boy who, in spite of an adventurous nature and the spirit of romance that was in him, loved a book better than a bat, solitude better than a crowd, his own companionship better than a mob of other lads. . . ."

Probably it was his love of both adventure and solitude that made him long to go to sea. He had read Jules Verne's *20,000 Leagues Under the Sea,* and he could imagine himself as Captain Nemo, commander of the *Nautilus* submarine. His father, on the other hand, hoped that Ernest would follow him into medicine. But in the end, Dr. Shackleton agreed to let his son go to sea. With ten children to raise, the doctor could not afford the cost of training Ernest as a naval cadet. Instead, he arranged for his son to sign on with a commercial sailing ship bound for South America. Ernest was 16.

Life on board a tall square-rigger meant hard work. Ernest had to climb high up in the ship's rigging to work the sails, even in bad weather and churning waves. "How would you like to be 150 feet up in the air; hanging on with one hand to a rope while with the other you try and get the sail in," Ernest wrote to a friend.

Despite the hardships and months at sea, Ernest loved the life of a merchant marine, a sailor on cargo ships. He also loved poetry and would often recite lines from Robert

Browning, his favorite poet, to his shipmates. "When he wasn't on duty on the deck he was stowed away in his cabin with his books," a shipmate remembered.

Ernest spent ten years as a merchant marine. He advanced quickly through the ranks, and by the time he was 24, he was qualified to command a British ship anywhere in the world. When he was on leave, he would come home to visit his family in the London suburbs. On one trip home in 1900, he heard about something called the National Antarctic Expedition. It was being organized by the Royal Geographical Society. The society had sent explorers to Africa and other parts of the globe, and now it wanted to send them to Antarctica.

Few people had ever seen that frigid, forbidding continent of ice, much less explored very far beyond its coastline. But the year before, a Norwegian named Carsten Borchgrevink had spent the winter in Antarctica and gone farther inland than anyone before him.

As an adult, Shackleton usually looked serious and unsmiling in pictures, but he was really a charming man who loved practical jokes. A boyhood picture of him at school (left) shows him wearing a faint smile. At 16 he left school to become a sailor.

The idea of exploring one of the world's last frontiers appealed to Ernest's imagination, and he applied to join the expedition. It would be led by Robert Falcon Scott, a young naval officer. In March 1901 his application was accepted. On the last day of July 1901, the expedition's ship, *Discovery,* sailed down England's River Thames with the 27-year-old Shackleton on board. By early January she had reached the southern seas that swirl around the white continent. Even though it was midsummer in the Southern Hemisphere, huge stretches of pack

"There is something curiously human about the manner and movement of these birds."

Trial By Ice

ice formed a dangerous floating belt around Antarctica. The sound of the ocean dashing against the ice floes, pushing them into one another, created a groaning that could be heard from far away. No noises of civilization broke the sounds of the polar wild: the roaring sea, the blowing hiss of whales, the squawking penguins and barking seals.

Scott was heading *Discovery* for the Ross Sea, and he had to thread carefully through the pack ice to get there. By January 9 the expedition was closing in on Antarctica, and the snow-clad continent's Admiralty Mountains were visible, rising from Cape Adare. Scott ordered a small landing party to go ashore, and Shackleton was one of the expedition's first members to stand on the shaly Antarctic ground. That ground was slick and foul smelling. Like almost any piece of ice-free land in Antarctica, it was inhabited by thousands of penguins who laid their eggs and raised their young there.

From Cape Adare *Discovery* continued south, passing under the frozen flanks of Mount Erebus, a volcano spouting a plume of smoke. Behind Erebus lay the Ross Ice Shelf, a floating field of ice as big as the state of Texas and as much as 2,000 feet thick.

Huge colonies of penguins live in Antarctica, and the young, like these emperor penguins, often huddle together in rookeries of thousands of birds. Although penguins can't fly in air, they seem to fly through the water. At left, an Adélie uses an icy ledge to launch itself for a deep dive.

Hoping to chart the unexplored coast of the Ross Sea, Scott followed the shoreline west, but *Discovery* was soon surrounded by pack ice and bergs. If the ship were to become trapped by sea ice, it could easily be crushed.

Although no one on board had much experience in polar seas, the crew managed to navigate *Discovery* through the ice safely. But it was clear she could not escape before the pack ice closed and froze her in for the season. The men of the National Antarctic Expedition would have to spend a long winter in the Antarctic. In those days there were no radios or computers to keep ships in touch with the rest of the world. *Discovery* and her men would be on their own.

Scott headed the ship for McMurdo Sound, a well-protected natural harbor on the Antarctic coast. The expedition would winter there. Then, when the brief southern summer came again, they would make a dash overland for the South Pole. Scott and the Royal Geographical Society wanted to plant the British flag at the southernmost spot on the globe.

Despite their hardiness and determination, the British team did not have the kind of equipment they needed for a race to the pole. Other polar pioneers, particularly the Norwegians who had explored the North Pole regions, had found that glacial ice and snow were best tackled on skis, with sleds and teams of dogs to haul equipment. The British had brought skis and dogs with them, but no one on the expedition was an expert with either. After trying unsuccessfully to control the sled dogs and learn to ski, they gave up. They decided instead to walk across the enormous frigid land.

After the British had been at McMurdo for 11 days, Scott appointed Shackleton commander of a three-man expedition to find a good route to start toward the Pole. Pulling a sled loaded with food and gear, Shackleton and his two companions set

Winter darkness and pack ice surround Discovery, *the ship Shackleton sailed on to Antarctica when he was 27. Trapped by ice,* Discovery *stayed in Antarctica a year longer than planned.*

Trial By Ice

out. Soon a gale began to blow. Antarctica is actually a desert and hardly ever receives any new precipitation, but winds whip old surface snow into driving blizzards. Now Shackleton and his men bent into the storm with all their might. At night they slept, wet and frozen, huddled together in a small tent. By day they struggled across the Ross Ice Shelf. One misstep could have plunged them to disaster, since a light dusting of snow often hid unseen crevasses—wide, deep cracks in glaciers—where a man could fall to his death.

Trial By Ice

"It is a unique sort of feeling to look on lands that have never been seen by human eyes before."

Shackleton's goal was a small outcropping of rock sticking up from the ice shelf. He made it there and back to McMurdo in four days. His short expedition didn't really accomplish much, but it did give him a taste for leadership. He found that he had a talent for commanding men, that they would trust their survival to him.

The problem was that Robert Scott, not Shackleton, was the commander of the expedition. Scott, too, could sense that Shackleton was a natural leader, and a rivalry began to grow between the two men. The long, dark months to come would only make it worse.

No sunshine reaches the Antarctic during the depths of winter, and the days passed without a glimmer of light. Other problems also plagued the men, particularly the fear of a disease called scurvy. It causes swollen gums and joints and keeps cuts from healing. After a while, it can lead to mental confusion and death.

Though its cause was then unknown, some scientists believed scurvy came from a lack of fresh food. (They were right. Scientists now know that scurvy is caused by

Early in the Discovery *expedition a few men, including Shackleton, inflated a hot-air balloon and made the first Antarctic balloon flight. Below,* Discovery *is caught by ice, while open water lies nearby.*

a lack of Vitamin C, found in fresh food.) Shackleton wanted Scott to feed the expedition seal meat, as seals were easy to find and would serve as a fresh food source. Scott did not like the idea and wanted to stick with the canned food the expedition had brought along. When some men began showing signs of scurvy, Scott finally agreed to change the diet.

As the daylight slowly returned and the men began to recover their health, thoughts turned to the race for the Pole. Scott planned to take just one man with him—Dr. Edward Wilson—but Wilson convinced Scott that they should also take Shackleton.

A polar explorer skis around pressure ridges that have formed hills of sheer ice. These huge cracked and jagged chunks of ice are squeezed up as plates of pack ice grind toward each other.

Though the Antarctic summer is blessed with long hours of sunlight, it lasts only a few weeks, and blizzards and wind storms can strike at any time. The three-man team would be racing against time, weather, and the threat of scurvy. Their main food would be "hoosh," a stew made of pemmican (ground dried meat) with hard biscuits crumbled in it.

On November 2 they started. This time they took dogs with them, though none of the three knew how to drive a dog team. They struggled along on foot in the snow. As they pushed forward, they left supplies of food buried along the way for their return trip.

Trial By Ice

They had unusually good weather for the first month, with few blizzards blowing up to create the blinding whiteouts that would force them to stop and wait. Still, they had covered only 109 miles by the beginning of December. The slow going meant their food was running low, and the dogs began to die of hunger and cold; some had to be killed. Shackleton himself was coughing a lot but still straining hard to pull a heavy sled. Now he and Scott, desperately hungry, cold, and exhausted, did not even pretend to respect each other. They also both had swollen gums, a sign of scurvy. Without fresh food they would only get weaker and sicker.

On Christmas Day both Shackleton and Wilson tried to persuade Scott to turn back. They had been out almost six weeks. It would take them that long to get back to the ship. And they were much too far from the South Pole to reach it. But Scott refused. They kept going forward till December 30. In the afternoon Shackleton stayed with the supplies, while the other two men continued a mile or two farther. They were measuring their progress not so much by miles as by latitude—imaginary lines that circle the globe from the Equator, at 0° latitude, to the Poles. The South Pole is at 90°S, and they had reached latitude 82°17'. That was to be their "Furthest South." Now, at last, Scott agreed to turn around and race for the ship.

It was a race for their lives. Supplies were desperately low, and the health and strength of the men, particularly Shackleton, were failing quickly. Though Shackleton tried to pull his share of the load, he began to cough up blood, and it was hard for him to breathe. Finally, Wilson, the doctor, forced him to stop pulling the sleds and follow on skis. For one afternoon Shackleton was so weak he had to ride on a sled. The humiliation of that would haunt him all his life.

After their race toward the South Pole in the winter of 1902, Shackleton, Robert Scott, and Dr. Edward Wilson returned to camp. They had traveled 200 miles farther south than any people before them, but that was still 450 miles short of the Pole.

Trial By Ice

"What a little speck on the snowy wilderness is our camp, all round white . . . and the sun shining down on it all."

On their last legs, the men got help from the wind. Roaring at their backs, it blew them across the barren Antarctic snows, and they made it to *Discovery* on February 3. One of the crew members described how strange the three men looked with their "long beards, hair, dirt, swollen lips & peeled complexions, & blood-shot eyes. . . ." The expedition was a disappointment. They had not succeeded in getting very close to the Pole, and they had come very close to losing their lives.

Shackleton's own sense of failure deepened when Scott ordered him home on a relief ship that had sailed into the open waters of McMurdo Sound, four miles away from the British base. *Discovery,* still locked in ice, would have to remain yet another year, until the ice melted the following austral, or southern, summer. Shackleton argued to stay, but Scott would not allow it. Officially, Scott wrote that he was ordering Shackleton's return "solely on account of his health." But Scott also resented Shackleton and his natural ability as a leader. From that time on, the two men would be rivals in a lifelong race to best each other at the Pole.

Straggling into camp after their three-month ordeal on the ice, Scott, Wilson, and Shackleton were met by shipmates relieved to see them safe. Shackleton, bringing up the rear, was suffering from scurvy and a weak heart.

"Never mind my beloved whether the days are dull or cold or dark, we will be all brightness and light in our little house. . . ."

When the disappointed Shackleton returned to England in 1903 at the age of 29, his longtime sweetheart, Emily Dorman, was waiting for him. She was a friend of his sisters whom he had met on leave when he was still a sailor. For several years he had been pouring his heart out to her in letters, telling her his thoughts and dreams. Emily understood Shackleton and his restless spirit well, saying about him, "One must not chain down an eagle in a barnyard." In April 1904 the two were married and soon settled in Edinburgh, Scotland, where Shackleton was running the offices of the Royal Scottish Geographical Society. With his usual charm and energy, Shackleton stormed through the society, making changes and exerting his natural influence as a leader. But after about a year, he found the work tedious, and he longed for something more exciting.

That would be the pattern of his life. He tried journalism, running for Parliament, and a number of exotic—and questionable—financial investments that he hoped would make him rich. But life in Britain never quite suited the adventuresome Anglo-Irishman. Ernest was simply bored by routine. And that lonely, windswept desert of ice and snow at the bottom of the world always called to him.

By 1907 Shackleton was deep in plans for his own expedition to the Pole. With the help of friends and admirers, he pieced together the money needed to fund it. When

When Ernest and Emily Shackleton's first child, Raymond, was born in 1905, Shackleton was said to have declared the baby had "good fists for fighting!"

Scott learned of the plans, he made Shackleton promise not to land at McMurdo Sound, claiming that part of the frozen continent for himself. No one had any claim to the continent, and Scott's request was unreasonable, but Shackleton reluctantly agreed to it.

The expedition ship, *Nimrod,* was a 41-year-old sealer from Newfoundland—not exactly the perfect vessel to take into the stormy southern oceans, but Shackleton, as always, was determined. Instead of the sled dogs he had found so troublesome on his previous polar expedition, he was taking small Manchurian ponies for transport, and a new invention, a motor car! As he sailed south, he wrote to Emily, "It gives me a lump in my throat when I think of my family."

By mid-January 1908 *Nimrod* was edging along the Antarctic coast, looking for a place on the Ross Ice Shelf called Barrier Inlet. But the inlet was gone! The ice that had formed it had calved, or broken away, from the main ice shelf and floated out to sea. The discovery shocked Shackleton, and he decided not to chance making a base on or near the unstable edge of the ice barrier. He began searching for another safe

Hauled up on the ice probably to sun itself, a seal seems more interested in the photographer taking its picture than in the contraption behind it—a Scottish motor car donated to the expedition. It proved useless on the ice.

Trial By Ice

landing spot, but he couldn't locate one. With no other choice, he headed *Nimrod* for McMurdo Sound. He would not risk the lives of his men to keep his promise to Scott. He wrote to his wife about his decision, saying, "My conscience is clear but my heart is sore. . . ."

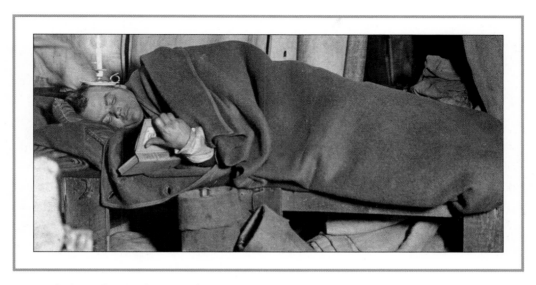

Tucked into his bunk on Nimrod, *George Marston, the expedition's artist, reads by the light of a carefully balanced candle. Like many others on* Nimrod, *Marston would follow Shackleton to Antarctica again aboard* Endurance.

Trial By Ice

At McMurdo Sound the expedition planned to set up a base at Hut Point, Scott's old camp. But pack ice blocked them. So they set up a base at nearby Cape Royds. They tried using the car to transfer supplies, but its tires could not get a good grip on the drifting snow. Once unloaded, *Nimrod* sailed back to New Zealand with orders to return in February 1909. For the next year the 13 men of the expedition would be on their own and out of contact with the rest of the world. They built a small hut, their only shelter from the weather, and settled in. Always concerned about keeping his men's spirits up, Shackleton ordered a small expedition to climb 12,448-foot Mount Erebus, where no human had set foot before. On March 10, after a five-day struggle, five men made it to the top. But winter was now closing in. Cramped together in the hut, the men talked, slept away the endless, tedious days, longed for home, and made plans for the run to the Pole.

Shackleton planned to take three men with him—Jameson Adams, Dr. Eric Marshall, and Frank Wild. In late August, when weak sunlight finally broke the endless Antarctic winter night, the men began laying in supplies at Hut Point, 20 miles away.

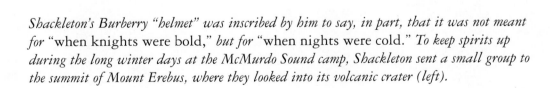

Shackleton's Burberry "helmet" was inscribed by him to say, in part, that it was not meant for "when knights were bold," *but for* "when nights were cold." *To keep spirits up during the long winter days at the McMurdo Sound camp, Shackleton sent a small group to the summit of Mount Erebus, where they looked into its volcanic crater (left).*

"At last we are out on the long trail after 4 years{'} thought and work."

At last, on October 29 with a bright sun shining in the blue polar sky, the adventure began. Since the car had failed, they used ponies to haul gear. The South Pole was about 750 treacherous miles away, and they had enough food for 91 days. That meant they had to cover an average of 16 miles a day—on foot.

After less than two weeks, the men realized the ponies were no good as polar pack animals. They could not stand the cold, and their heavy weight broke through the snow, sometimes sending them plunging down crevasses. In the end, all of the ponies died. Their carcasses provided the men with much-needed fresh meat to ward off scurvy. Once again Shackleton found himself and his men pulling heavy sleds toward the South Pole.

Shackleton had hoped that a vast plain of snow and ice lay between him and his goal. But he was wrong. The high, jagged Transantarctic Mountains stood in his path. But luck was on his side. In early December he and his men came upon one of the few passes through the mountains. A glacier they called the Golden Gateway led them to a stupendous ice field 30 miles wide and more than 100 miles long. Wild

believed that it "must be the largest in the world. . . ." Though deep snow, crevasses, and other obstacles marred its glistening blue surface, still it beckoned like a wide road, and Shackleton and his men took it.

A week later they were still climbing the glacier, scrambling over high ridges of ice, roped together to keep from falling into hidden crevasses. As they climbed higher, the cold and wind grew worse, and frostbite threatened their fingers, toes, and faces. They were running low on food and had little fuel left either to cook with or to melt snow for drinking water. Yet they kept going, and by December 28 they at last left the glacier behind and became the first humans ever to set foot on the smooth, vast ice cap that covers the South Pole.

With each passing day, cold and hunger gnawed at them. Shackleton now had to admit that he would not reach the Pole itself, but he was determined to get within a hundred miles of it. Finally, on January 9, Marshall, the expedition navigator, calculated that they were 88°23' south, about 97 miles from the Pole. They had beaten Scott's Furthest South—by 360 miles!

Shackleton agreed now to turn around, but hundreds of miles lay between the men and the safety of Hut Point. Along the way, they had to locate the food depots that they had left for their return trip. At one point, they had nothing to eat for 40 hours. They were in a race to survive.

None of the ponies Shackleton used for his 1908 race to the Pole survived. They sank into the snow instead of gliding on it, and they were always cold and hungry. Shackleton and his men spent valuable hours caring for them.

"The Pole is hard to get, but we will, Please God get there."

While the four men were struggling toward Hut Point, *Nimrod* had returned to McMurdo Sound. The captain had orders to wait for Shackleton and his men until March 1. After that, he should consider them lost and sail back to New Zealand. On February 28, as the ship waited, everyone on board believed that the men had died. Then, on March 1, they spotted two tiny figures waving a flag at Hut Point. It was Shackleton and Wild! They had struggled ahead to make it in time.

Once again Shackleton had failed to reach the Pole, but to Emily he wrote, "Though I may be disappointed I will come back to the loving arms . . . of you my wife and in the joy of seeing you . . . and our children all will be forgotten." And once again, too, he had proved his leadership. All his men returned to England safely, and Shackleton was hailed as a hero. To honor him as a great adventurer of the age, King Edward VII knighted him Sir Ernest Shackleton.

Four men from Nimrod*(left to right)—Frank Wild, Shackleton, Eric Marshall, and Jameson Adams—set a new "Furthest South" record, coming within 97 miles of the Pole.*

On December 14, 1911, a Norwegian party (top), led by famous polar explorer Roald Amundsen, won the race to the South Pole. At the same time, Robert Scott (below, center, standing), was leading his own polar expedition. All five men on it perished.

The very next year a Norwegian party led by Roald Amundsen did what Shackleton had failed to do. On December 14, 1911, they reached the South Pole. Although Shackleton had lost the race to the Pole, he was still haunted by the Antarctic world. Now 39 years old, he began planning a third expedition to Antarctica. He had a new goal: to cross the entire continent, a journey of 1,500 miles. This would mean using two ships. One group would go with him to the Weddell Sea. Shackleton named this ship, a Norwegian polar ship, *Endurance,* after his family motto: "By endurance we conquer."

On the way south to Antarctica in 1914, Endurance *put in at the whaling station on South Georgia Island to buy provisions. Frank Hurley, the expedition's photographer, persuaded a few shipmates to help him lug his heavy camera gear up a mountaintop for a shot down on* Endurance *at anchor in the harbor. Little did the men know what role the island would eventually play in their fate.*

After landing, they would make the overland crossing in what Shackleton hoped would be a hundred days. This time he would use sled dogs. Meanwhile, a second ship, *Aurora,* would sail to the Ross Sea at the opposite side of the continent. A land party from the ship would lay supply depots a hundred miles into the interior so that Shackleton and his party would have food when they neared the far side of the continent. Once they reached the coast of the Ross Sea, *Aurora* would pick them up.

Just as the two ships sailed from Europe in 1914, fighting broke out between England and Germany. The First World War had begun. The men aboard *Endurance* had no idea how much this would change the world they were leaving behind.

As always, the two Antarctic-bound ships planned to arrive at their destinations during the austral summer so they would have time to establish bases before winter set in. But when *Endurance* neared the continent in mid-December, unseasonable pack ice forced her to push her way slowly through the Weddell Sea. On January 19 the sound of the battering suddenly stopped. *Endurance* was caught by the ice and held tight. Around her the sea was frozen in every direction as far as the eye could see. The ship was only a day's sail from the landing base Shackleton had been aiming for, but now he was helpless. He had no choice but to drift with the pack.

Endurance *used steam power to thread her way through the ice. Built for polar seas, the 144-foot-long ship could shove through loose ice, "shattering the floes in grand style."*

Trial By Ice

"Pack-ice might be described as a gigantic and interminable jigsaw puzzle devised by nature."

After almost a month of being helplessly frozen in, the men saw a gash of open water just a few hundred yards from the ship. Shackleton sent a group out with saws to try to hack a channel in the ice from the ship to the open water. They sawed away, but in places the ice was 18 feet thick. The job was impossible. Although open water was close, they could not get *Endurance* to it. They would have to wait for the ice to break up on its own.

By March, winter was setting in. The currents and winds changed back and forth, sometimes pushing them south toward Antarctica, and sometimes pushing them away from the continent and into unknown seas. Through it all, Shackleton remained the calm, cheerful leader who was affectionately called "Boss" by his men.

Working frantically, the men tried to cut a lead through the ice for Endurance *(left). Warmed by the ship's stove, shipmates keep the night watchman company.*

To pass the long, boring days, the 29 men aboard *Endurance* played parlor games like animal, vegetable, mineral, or they impersonated one another or sang songs.

In early August the pack ice at last began to break up. But Shackleton and a few others realized that, far from escape, this might mean the death of *Endurance*. Frozen in place the ship was safe, but now the grinding, unstable pressure ridges of ice,

80

A stowaway who became ship steward, 19-year-old Perce Blackborow poses with the expedition's cat, Mrs. Chippy. Angry that Blackborow had snuck aboard his ship, Shackleton gruffly told the young sailor, "the first person we eat will be you." Leonard Hussey (far left) hoists sled dog Samson. At times the men played soccer on the frozen pack ice that held Endurance *fast.*

which looked like frozen waves, could squeeze the ship. By late October *Endurance* was caught in a vise of ice that buckled her seams and allowed the frigid ocean water to seep in. The men fought hard to save her by pumping out the water, but it was no good. On October 27 her timbers creaked and groaned, and her beams cracked.

Trial By Ice

"What the ice takes, the ice keeps."

"It was a pitiful sight," one expedition member wrote. "To all of us she seemed like a living thing . . . and it was awful to witness her torture."

Shackleton ordered the men to abandon ship, move their gear out onto an ice floe, and set up tents for shelter. Now they were shipless, floating they knew not where on an enormous moving island of ice, and no one in the world knew where they were.

Shackleton never believed in giving up. Soon the Boss had a plan. The men would march 312 miles across the floes to an old Swedish base at Snow Hill, where there would probably be some supplies. From there, Shackleton would take a small party another 130 miles overland to Wilhelmina Bay, a place whalers often patrolled. But his plan had a problem. The floe ice was mushy, and the men sank in with every step. Hauling heavy sleds full of gear was almost impossible. After a while, they stopped

Sled dogs watch as Endurance *is crushed by ice. "She was doomed: no ship built by human hands could have withstood the strain," Shackleton wrote. Hauling lifeboats and sleds over pack ice, the men tried to reach a hut 312 miles away, but the going was too hard.*

"*Living in a tent without any furniture requires a little getting used to.*"

trying and set up a base they called Ocean Camp. It was November 1, 1915.

To ward off scurvy, the men hunted seal and penguin for food. They used blubber—fat from the seals—as fuel for cooking and to melt ice for drinking water. In the evenings they played cards and sang to keep their spirits up.

In late December the pack ice began to break up, and Shackleton moved camp. But again the going was very tough, and the men did not get far before settling onto another floe they called Patience Camp. The ice was being blown east then west

Shackleton (left) and Frank Wild survey the scene at Ocean Camp, where the men spent two months. Set up on pack ice about a mile and a half from the wreck of Endurance, *the camp's location allowed the men to go back to the ship and salvage supplies from it.*

by the winds and currents, and the men could do nothing but wait. By late March 1916, after five months on the ice, their camp floe was getting dangerously thin.

Then suddenly, they spotted land in the distance. It was Joinville Island, at the tip of the Antarctic Peninsula. But they couldn't reach it, and they now realized that they were being swept out of the Weddell Sea into the open ocean. Their floe had shrunk to a small island only big enough for their camp. And it was beginning to disintegrate beneath their feet. On April 9 Shackleton knew they had to abandon the floe. They crowded into three boats they had dragged with them from *Endurance* and set out on the stormy southern seas.

Weaving through drifting pack ice, they rowed and sailed all day, then pulled up on a long floe at night to rest. About 11 p.m. Shackleton felt uneasy and got up to check on things. As he walked across the floe, the ice suddenly cracked under his feet and ran under a tent up ahead, tipping a man in his sleeping bag into the frigid water. Shackleton quickly pulled him back onto the floe, just before the crack snapped shut again! The man struggled out of his bag, "wet but otherwise unscathed." No one slept the rest of that night.

The next day, it was back in the boats. And the next and the next and the next. Waves sent freezing water hurling over the men, turning their clothes to ice. They were always wet and cold, and the rough waters often made them seasick. They had no drinking water, so they were forever thirsty. They didn't know when—or if—they would sight land again.

When Endurance *went down, Shackleton (left) said to his men, "Ship and stores have gone—so now we'll go home." Despite the desperate situation, the men never lost faith in his leadership. A map Shackleton sketched on the back of a menu card (right) shows his planned trek across Antarctica in 1914.*

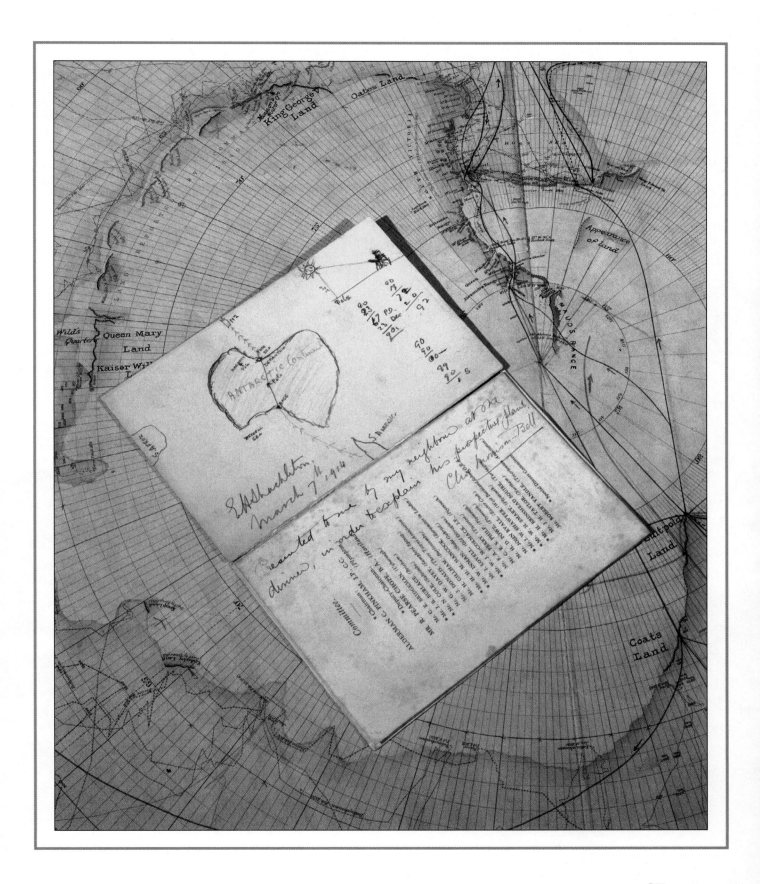

Then, after six days, they saw land ahead! It was Elephant Island, an uninhabited place with sheer cliffs pounded by waves. At first they could find no landing spot, and for another day they were stuck at sea as they circled the island, looking for a safe place to beach the boats. At last they landed on a narrow, rocky beach. "Conceive our joy on setting foot on solid earth after 170 days of life on a drifting ice floe . . . ," the expedition's photographer, Hurley, wrote. The men heated milk and drank a toast to their success.

Shackleton had brought all his men safely across raging southern seas. Now he had to get them, somehow, back to civilization. He decided his only choice was to cross more ocean. A whaling station run by Norwegians lay on the island of South Georgia, more than 700 treacherous miles away. It was a small dot in the vast sea. But he would have to sail there.

Trial By Ice

After a harrowing ocean crossing, the men reached uninhabited Elephant Island. In his picture of the landing (below), photographer Hurley drew an iceberg in the background. For four months, 22 men lived on the island in a hut roofed by two overturned boats.

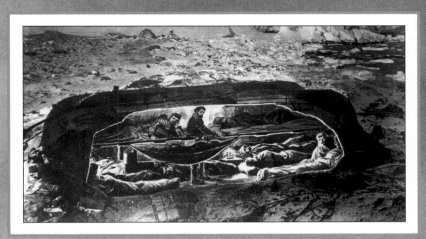

89

"The men who were staying behind made a pathetic little group on the beach, with . . . the sea seething at their feet. . . ."

On April 24, a week after the group had arrived on Elephant Island, Shackleton and five other men pushed off in the 22-foot-long *James Caird*. Of all the hardships they had already managed to survive, they knew this journey would be their toughest challenge. And it was. Gales blew against them, and ice caked on them and on the canvas sheet that covered part of their boat. They took turns sleeping, a few at a time crawling into the narrow bow space under the canvas, where reindeer hair from their sleeping bags got into their noses and eyes. Heavy seas broke their anchor line, so they could not stop. At one point a wave as high as a four-story building broke over the boat, and the men bailed frantically to keep from sinking. And all the while, they worried that they might sweep past South Georgia without ever seeing it and be lost in the endless ocean.

As Shackleton and five others set out again in the James Caird *(above,) the men left on Elephant Island waved a hearty farewell. "The* Caird *is an excellent sailer, & . . . should make Sth. Georgia in 14 days," Hurley predicted. It took 17 days "of supreme strife," Shackleton later wrote.*

Trial By Ice

Trial By Ice

> *"The mountains peered through the mists, and between them huge glaciers poured down the great ice-slopes which lay behind."*

But their navigator, Worsley, somehow managed to keep them on track. And, just after noon on May 8, there it was! The very island they had been aiming for. But just as at Elephant Island, surf pounded against mean, steep cliffs, making landing impossible. To make matters worse, a hurricane was shrieking in on top of them. So, with land in view and their thirst parching them, they had to wait. Finally, after two days of struggling against the weather and searching for a landing spot, they beached the *James Caird* in a small cove. But the ordeal was not over. The whaling station lay on the far side of the island. They had to cross the mountains and glaciers that covered the interior of South Georgia.

After resting for a few days, Shackleton, Frank Worsley, and Thomas Crean made a dash for the far side of the island. They took no sleeping bags, and each man carried his food in three socks tied around his neck so his hands would be free to climb. Several times as they labored up and down the snow-clad mountains, they got lost and had to retrace their steps, even though they were bone tired. On one steep snowy slope, the men took a chance and slid down. "For a moment my hair stood on end,"

"Savage and horrible," the world-navigating explorer Captain James Cook called South Georgia 140 years before Shackleton arrived.

Worsley later wrote. "Then . . . quite suddenly . . . I was actually enjoying it." So were Shackleton and Crean.

Finally, after more than 24 hours of constant climbing and their strength failing them, they spotted the whaling station below. Hurrying in that direction, they found a waterfall in their way. But they weren't going to be slowed now. They slid down it using a rope, as they had slid down the snow slope, and kept walking. Their "dash" had taken 36 hours, but now help was really at hand.

They straggled into the whaling station looking like wild men, their eyes bloodshot,

Trial By Ice

their faces burned dark by wind, sun, and soot from blubber fires. Two little boys saw them and ran away, frightened. The boss of the whaling station had known Shackleton before and recognized his voice. He welcomed them and fed them breads, cakes, and other treats they had not had for more than a year and a half.

At the Grytviken whaling station on South Georgia, Norwegian workers begin to flense—or strip blubber from—a whale. The stench of whale flesh filled the air in these stations, all of which are now closed.

"We had pierced the veneer of outside things. We had suffered, starved and triumphed. . . ."

As nice as it was to be back in civilization, Shackleton was anxious to rescue his men. That same night the station boss sent a boat to pick up the men on the other side of South Georgia. That part was easy, but it would be a long, hard struggle to get the men back from Elephant Island.

Shackleton tried four times in four different boats to get through the pack ice around the island. The fourth time he finally made it in a Chilean ship called *Yelcho.* It was August 28, 1916. It had been 126 days since Shackleton had set sail in *James Caird,* and the men left on the island were beginning to lose hope.

Despite all the months of cold, hunger, and wet, not a single man had been lost. When his wife, Emily, heard that he and his men were safe, she said, "I am so thankful that he rescued his men . . . instead of being *fetched.*"

After the rescue and return of Shackleton and his crew from the Endurance *exploration, his wife, Emily Shackleton, was happy to have her husband home alive.*

"A curious piece of ice on the horizon . . . bore a striking resemblance to a ship," one of the men on Elephant Island recalled, as the Chilean ship Yelcho came within sight. The men lit a fire to attract the ship's attention, and soon Shackleton was rowing ashore to rescue them.

"Sometimes I think I am no good at anything but being away in the wilds. . . ."

But there was one more rescue to be made before Shackleton could rest. The group of men from the ship *Aurora* had been stranded for more than two years at McMurdo Sound while the *Aurora* itself was stuck in Australia, plagued by weather and financial problems. Shackleton now had to sail halfway around the world to Australia and then take *Aurora* to Antarctica. When he picked up the survivors, he found that two of the men were missing, and one had died. Though Shackleton searched for the missing men for days, he found no trace of them.

When at last Shackleton returned home to England and his wife and children, the First World War was still raging. He wanted to do his part, and for a while he helped organize troops and supplies amid the arctic cold of northern Russia. But when the war was over, he was once again bored with everyday life. He began planning another expedition, this one to circle the entire Antarctic continent by ship. Many of the men from *Endurance* wanted to go with him. To them, he was forever the Boss—the greatest leader and hero they had ever known.

In December 1921 they steamed south once again, and by early January their ship, *Quest,* was in South Georgia. But Shackleton's health was failing. Since his very first expedition with Scott, he had suspected that he had a weak heart. Now, at last, it gave out. On January 5, 1922, the Boss died. He was 47 years old. "We would have gone anywhere without question just on his order . . . ," one of his men wrote. "Now that he is gone, there is a gap in our lives that can never be filled."

His wife, Emily, decided that her husband should be buried on South Georgia, and that is where Shackleton lies today—amid the wild glaciers and roaring gales of the southern lands he loved so well.

Aboard Quest, *Shackleton made the final journey of his life—back to the Antarctic. Revisiting the whaling station on South Georgia, he regained some of his old enthusiasm, though in his diary he confessed, "I grow old and tired but must always lead on."*

The men aboard Quest *left their picture and signatures buried in a bottle at the foot of Shackleton's grave on South Georgia. Many of them had been with the Boss on* Endurance *as well, and to them he was the leader they would never forget. Their "message in a bottle" was discovered only in recent years.*

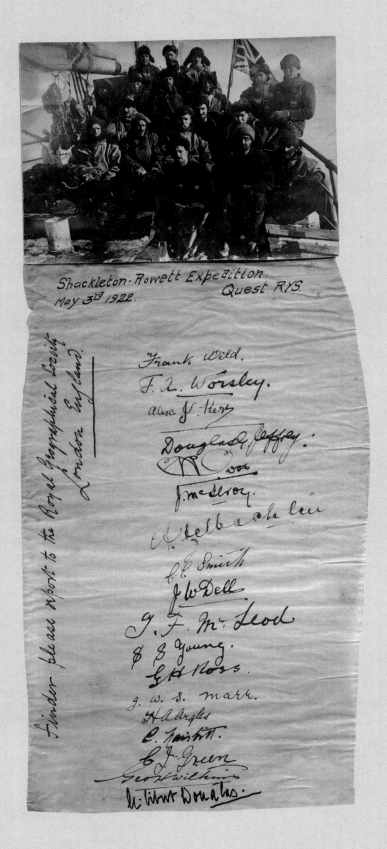

Shackleton-Rowett Expedition.
May 3rd 1922.   Quest R.Y.S.

Finder please report to the Royal Geographical Society, London England.

Frank Wild.
F. A. Worsley.
Alex J. Kerr
Douglas Jeffrey.
J. McIlroy.
A. Aelbachelin
C. E. Smith
J. W. Dell
G. F. Mc Leod
S. S. Young.
G. H. Ross.
G. W. S. Mark.
H. A. Argles
C. Naisbitt.
C. J. Green
George Wilkins
Wilbert Douglas.

AFTERWORD

Ernest Shackleton never stood at the South Pole. He never circumnavigated Antarctica. He never achieved the goals he set for himself. He lived not quite 48 years and died exhausted, dispirited, and in debt. Yet he always followed his dreams. "I shall go on going . . . till one day I shall not come back," he said near the end of his life. Like many people whose accomplishments have won them lasting fame and admiration, Shackleton did not realize what he had contributed to humankind.

Yet now he is considered one of the greatest explorers and natural leaders the world has ever known. His name has become so synonymous with bravery and endurance that when other explorers set out on their own quests, they sometimes simply say the name—Shackleton—to give them courage. Even today, the story of *Endurance* is one of the world's great tales of adventure. Most people, finding themselves helplessly adrift on ice at the end of the Earth, would simply give up. But not Shackleton. "Never the lowered Banner/Never the lost Endeavor," he proclaimed. His calm confidence, unfailing optimism, and selfless leadership inspired his men to believe that they all could—and would—survive.

Surviving against the odds was his talent, and he preferred the simple ferocity of Antarctica, where the fight for survival was a daily challenge, to the disappointments, intrigues, and routines of the civilized world. "Courage and willpower can make miracles," Shackleton's friend and fellow polar explorer Roald Amundsen said of him, adding, "I know of no better example than what that man has accomplished."

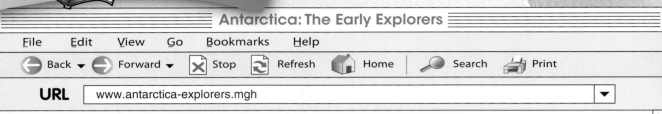

Beyond the Book

File   Edit   View   Go   Bookmarks   Help

← Back ▾   → Forward ▾   ☒ Stop   ⟳ Refresh   🏠 Home   🔍 Search   🖨 Print

URL   www.antarctica-explorers.mgh   ▾

| Home | Explorers | **Illness and Injury** | Milestones | Tragedies | Reference | Games |

You are here: Home / Illness and Injury

Search   [   ] go

Barely Surviving a World of Ice

By Mira Hawkins

Imagine a landscape that freezes the moisture in your eyes, that numbs your fingers in mere seconds, and that oftentimes goes days—weeks—with no sunshine. In this landscape, plant life is nearly nonexistent, and the animals that do survive have layers of fat that keeps them warm. A couple hundred years ago, mountains of ice and crevasses of darkness watched and waited as brave explorers traveled slowly across Antarctica. If the cold didn't kill the travelers, starvation or scurvy could have. If illness didn't kill them, frostbite or falls into chasms could have. Here, read about the illnesses and injuries that befell many Antarctic explorers in the 1800s and early 1900s.

HYPOTHERMIA

In the far-below-zero temperatures of Antarctica, explorers without proper clothing soon perished from hypothermia. When the body drops below 89 degrees Fahrenheit, shivering stops, skin turns blue, and extreme confusion sets in, followed by death.

STARVATION

After eight to ten weeks with little or no food, the human body shuts down and eventually dies. Antarctic explorers often ran out of food or ate so little that their bodies gave out. Several explorers starved to death on their ships or before they could get back to camp.

SUFFOCATION

Some explorers fell asleep in their tents and suffocated during the night. How? Their tents became encased in falling snow or were smothered by an **avalanche**. Explorers often ran out of air only four or five feet below the surface.

SCURVY

Sailors at sea for extended periods of time sometimes ran out of fruits and vegetables, which contain **vitamin C**. When the body doesn't get enough vitamin C, scurvy sets in—and brings fatigue, bleeding gums, and a rash on the legs.

FROSTBITE

In extreme cold, blood vessels close to the skin constrict as the body tries to keep its core temperature from falling. The areas of the body farthest from the heart—fingers, toes, nose, and ears—are most prone. Frostbitten areas eventually become numb and turn black. Many times frostbite leads to **amputation**.

Frostbite

POISONING

In the 1800s, canned foods were a new way to keep food fresh on years-long sea voyages. However, these first canned foods used **lead lids**, which caused lead poisoning (confusion and muscle weakness). Further, sometimes the food inside the cans wasn't cooked long enough before the cans were sealed. This led to food poisoning or sometimes **botulism** (difficulty swallowing and eventually paralysis and death).

13% of 36K

Extension Activity

Connecting with a Character: Ernest Shackleton and Robert Scott were rivals in a lifelong race to get to the South Pole. (a) Explain this rivalry, and discuss two ways Scott had an impact on Shackleton's life. (b) Think of someone who has had an impact in this way on your life. Describe this person and two ways this person has affected you. (c) Write a summary of your paper.

Paper Requirements: Paper must begin with a title page that lists the paper's title, your name, and the date. Paper must be two or three pages long (not including the title page).

Also By The Author

If you enjoyed *Trial by Ice,* you may enjoy these other books authored or coauthored by K. M. Kostyal:

- *Art of the State: Virginia* (nonfiction; a look at Virginia's treasures of past and present)
- *Birds* (nonfiction; part of the National Geographic Nature Library)
- *Field of Battle: The Civil War Letters of Major Thomas J. Halsey* (nonfiction)
- *Stonewall Jackson: A Life Portrait* (nonfiction; a biography of the Civil War legend Thomas "Stonewall" Jackson)

Related Topics

If you enjoyed the topics discussed in *Trial by Ice,* you may enjoy these other books that explore similar topics:

- *Emperors of the Ice: A True Story of Disaster and Survival in the Antarctic, 1910–13* by Richard Farr (nonfiction; account of Apsley George Benet Cherry-Garrard's battle with the elements as he embarks on a journey to collect emperor penguin eggs)
- *Explorers: The Most Exciting Voyages of Discovery—From the African Expeditions to the Lunar Landing* by Andrea de Porti (nonfiction; chronicles fifty-eight expeditions; uses a mix of rare photographs, travel narratives, and biographies)
- *Sea Cows, Shamans, and Scurvy: Alaska's First Naturalist: Georg Wilhelm Steller* by Ann Arnold (nonfiction; account of Steller's America-bound journey from Siberia)
- *Shipwreck at the Bottom of the World: The Extraordinary True Story of Shackleton and the Endurance* by Jennifer Armstrong (nonfiction; about Shackleton and his crew members)

PRINCESS OF THE PRESS

The Story of Ida B. Wells-Barnett

Angela Shelf Medearis

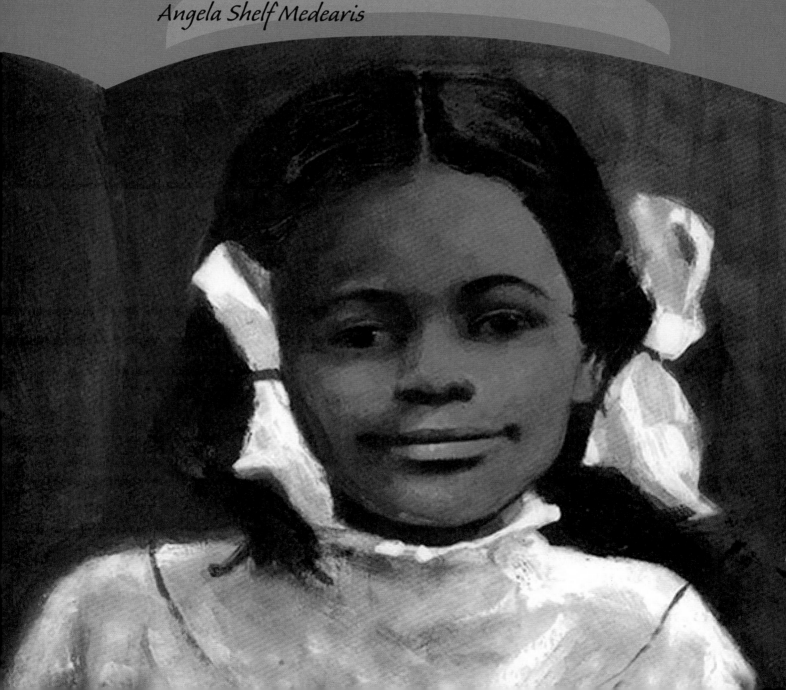

1

A Letter From Home

On a cool fall day in 1876, Ida Bell Wells scrubbed the pans left from the morning dishes. She was paying a visit to her grandmother Wells's farm, and had only recently recovered from a bout of chills and fever. Ida was still feeling a little ill, and she was also homesick. She missed her parents and her little brothers and sisters. Her mother, Lizzie, was one of the best cooks in the county. Her father, Jim, was a wonderful carpenter and shared Ida's love for reading the news and also enjoyed hearing Ida read aloud. Jim was also active in the Republican party and often discussed the power of the vote and current events with Ida. [1]

Ida's brother Jim Jr. was eleven, George was nine, and chubby little Stanley, her baby brother, was nine months old. Another brother, Eddie, had died of spinal meningitis when Ida was a little girl. Her sister, Eugenia, who was eleven, had been physically disabled for the last seven years with a disease that left her spine twisted and her legs without feeling. Although Eugenia was often ill and unable to walk, she was one of Ida's closest friends and playmates. Ida also wondered what her pesky little sisters, five-year-old Annie and two-year-old Lillie, were doing. Ida was fourteen and the oldest, so she often helped her parents take care of her younger brothers and sisters. She missed the noise and the laughter that filled their house in Holly Springs, Mississippi. Ida's parents worked hard to make sure all of their children were loved and cared for. They wanted them to have a better life than their own.[2]

Both of Ida's parents had been born into slavery. Jim's father was a slave owner who had purchased Jim's mother, Peggy. Jim was his only son. Master Wells would not allow Jim to be mistreated and made sure he had a good education. As soon as he turned eighteen, Jim was apprenticed to Mr. Bolling, a local carpenter, so that he could learn a skill. Ida's mother, Lizzie, was Mr. Bollings's cook. Jim and Lizzie fell in love, and a slave marriage was performed.

Unlike Ida's father, her mother had been cruelly treated as a slave. When they were children, Lizzie and her sister, Belle, were separated from their family and sold from one mean owner to the next. Lizzie spent her life trying to locate the rest of her family without success.[3]

The Civil War started in 1861. In 1863, President Abraham Lincoln issued the Emancipation Proclamation, which freed the slaves in the Confederate states. Ida was six months old. By 1865, the North had defeated the South, and slavery came to an end everywhere in America. The Southern states started to rebuild, and a period called Reconstruction began. During this time, African-American men had the right to vote, and African-Americans could start their own businesses. Jim and Lizzie remarried as a free man and woman, determined to build a good life for themselves and for their family.

The Freedmen's Aid Society started a school for the newly freed slaves—Shaw University. Like many former slaves who had been denied the chance to learn, Jim and Lizzie valued education. Jim became a trustee at the university, and Ida was one of the first children to attend the school. Ida excelled in all her classes, and was far ahead of the other students. Lizzie attended classes at Shaw University five days a week, along with Ida and the rest of the children. She had never learned to read or write because it was against the law for slaves to be educated. One of Lizzie's proudest moments was when she was finally able to read the Bible by herself.

Saturdays were a busy time at the Wells's house. Ida spent the day helping her mother with the cleaning. Her father and brother made sure everyone's shoes were polished. Lizzie and Ida pressed clothes, bathed the younger children, and washed their hair. Ida helped her mother prepare Sunday dinner so that it would be ready for them to eat after church. Every Sunday morning, the Wells family sat on a wooden pew side by side. Once, the Wellses received the prize for perfect attendance for a year.[4]

Ida sighed as she dried the dishes. At first, she had been looking forward to visiting her grandmother. She thought it would be fun to leave her regular chores and her baby-sitting duties and get away for a while. Now she wished she was back at home. A few days after Ida arrived at her grandmother's house, she received the news that a horrible epidemic of yellow fever was sweeping through Memphis, Tennessee, which was about fifty miles away from Holly Springs. The mayor of Holly Springs had refused to quarantine the town, and the fever had spread there. This same disease had killed many people three years earlier. Ida hoped that her family had left town and escaped the sickness, but she wasn't sure. The mail didn't come very often to Grandmother Wells's farm, and Ida hadn't heard from her family in several days.

As Ida stacked the dishes in the cabinet, she heard a knock at the front door. She smiled when she recognized three men who were friends of her parents. The men sat down in the living room and looked solemnly at Ida. One of them handed her a letter. It was from Ida's next-door neighbor. Ida hoped that the letter would contain some news about her family.

As Ida quickly read the first page, she grew more and more frightened. Many people had died from the yellow fever that had swept through the town, and hundreds were sick. As Ida turned the page, one terrible paragraph leapt out at her: "Jim and Lizzie Wells both died of yellow fever within twenty-four hours of each other. The children are all at home and the Howard Association has put a woman there to take care of them. Send word to Ida."[5]

Ida couldn't believe that her parents were dead. She sat numbly for what seemed like hours. Her grandmother, who had been joined by her aunt and uncle, tried to comfort her, but Ida didn't respond to what they were saying. She was worried about her younger brothers and sisters and wondered how they were doing. She knew that the woman from the Howard Association would take good care of them until she arrived.

The Howard Association was a charity of which her father had been a member. The association took care of the sick and orphaned.

In order to stop the spread of yellow fever, Ida's parents would be buried immediately. Ida would not be able to attend the funeral. She was heartbroken.

Like many young women of her time, Ida kept a diary. Her diary was like a good friend, a place she could write down her thoughts, hopes, and fears. It made Ida feel better to write down everything that was happening to her. "I wanted to go home at once," Ida wrote in her diary after learning about her parents' deaths. "But not until three days later, on the receipt of a letter from the doctor in charge [from the Howard Association], who said I ought to come home, were they willing to let me go." She continued:

> When my uncle and I got to the next railroad town, from which I was to take the train to Holly Springs, all the people in that station urged me not to go. They were sure that coming from the country I would fall victim [to the fever] at once, and that it was better for me to stay away until the epidemic was over, so that I could take care of the children, if any were left. . . . I consented to stay there and write home. But when I thought of my crippled sister [Eugenia], of the smaller children all down to my nine-month-old baby brother, the conviction grew within me that I ought to be with them.[6]

Ida went back to the railroad station, determined to return home. Because of the yellow fever, no passenger trains were available, so Ida paid to ride on a freight train that normally hauled cargo and animals. The train was draped with black cloth, because two of the conductors had recently died from yellow fever. The remaining conductor told Ida she was making a mistake and that she should stay in the country.

"Why are you running the train when you know you will probably get the fever?" Ida asked the conductor.

"Someone has to do it," he replied.

"That's exactly why I am going home," Ida told him. "I am the oldest of seven children. There's nobody but me to look after them now. Don't you think I should do my duty too?" The conductor didn't say anything else, but Ida knew that he thought she would probably catch the fever and die. When the train reached Holly Springs, he waved good-bye to Ida as though he would never see her again.[7]

2

We Will Not Be Separated

When Ida finally arrived at her home, she found out that Stanley, her baby brother, had died from the fever, and that all of the children, except her sister Eugenia, were sick. The family doctor scolded Ida and told her that she shouldn't have come home, but Eugenia was happy to see her.

"When the fever first broke out, we couldn't leave because there was no room for us at Aunt Belle's house," Eugenia told Ida. "Father went about his work, nursing the sick and making coffins for the dead. He sent us food and money, but he would not come home at night for fear of spreading the sickness to us. Then Mother got the fever, and Father came to help nurse her. He came down with the fever, too, and died the day before she did."[1]

Eugenia began to cry. Ida put her arms around her sister and hugged her tightly.

"Everything will be all right," Ida said. "I'm home now."

The next day, Ida began to feel ill and trembled with chills and fever. The nurse who was tending to the other children also took care of Ida. Ida was ill for four days, but slowly she began to recover. As soon as she felt strong enough, Ida went into town to take care of the family business.

After their father died, Eugenia had given Doctor Gray, who was assigned to the family from the Howard Association, three hundred dollars to lock in a safe. Eugenia knew that Dr. Gray would be leaving town soon, and she was anxious to get the money from him before he left. Eugenia wrote Dr. Gray a note and gave it, along with the receipt for the money, to Ida to deliver to him.

The town was crowded with people, and Ida wasn't sure who Dr. Gray was. She asked someone to point him out to her. When she told Dr. Gray who she was he smiled.

"So you are Genie's big sister," Dr. Gray said. "Tell her the treasurer has the key to the safe, and he is out in the country to see his family. He will be back this evening, and I will bring her the money tonight, as I am leaving tomorrow. You children had a wonderful father. He was one of the best aides in helping us with the sick. He'd be passing through the courthouse on his way to the shop; if a patient was restless, he would stop to quiet him, if he were dying he would talk to him or pray with him, then pick up his tools and go on with the rest of the day's work. Everyone liked him, and we all missed him when he was gone."[2]

Ida smiled and thanked him. The three hundred dollars would not go very far, but it would help buy food, medicine, and clothing for her family until Ida could think of a way to take care of them all.

As soon as the yellow fever epidemic was over, a meeting was scheduled to discuss the children's future. That evening, Ida hurriedly gave her little sisters a bath and put them to bed. Then she helped Eugenia get comfortable for the night. The two boys weren't ready to go to sleep yet, so Ida allowed them to sit out on the front steps. Ida could hear the boys talking quietly to each other. Then she waited for her father's friends to arrive for the meeting.

Ida's father had belonged to a group called the Masons, a charitable brotherhood that took care of the needs of its members. The Masons wanted to help and protect Ida and her brothers and sisters. After everyone had arrived, the men talked among themselves about what should be done with the children. They discussed each child almost as if Ida weren't there.

"We've always wanted a young'un of our own," Brother Gresham said. "The Lord never blessed us, so we would love to have little Lillie. She is only two, and we could raise her as our own."

"And Annie is just about the age of our Dorothy and would be right smart company for her," Brother Dobbs said. "Martha and I will take Annie."

"Jim and George can go with Henry Allen," Brother Miller said. "He is a carpenter, too, and has said he will give the boys a home. Jim is eleven now and can drive a nail straight as his daddy used to. George is almost as good, even though he is only nine. You know, Big Jim spent lots of time teaching them, and nobody could have put up a better fence than that one outside, and many a grown man couldn't have done as well."

The Wellses' house was small and neat, and a picket fence surrounded a lovely flower bed that had been the pride and joy of Ida's mother.

"Poor Eugenia," Brother Hall said. "What can we do about Eugenia? She can't do nothing but sit in her chair all day. Everybody I talked to said it was best to send her to the poorhouse. They can care for her there better than anywhere else, and her so sickly too."

No one came up with a better solution or offered Eugenia a home, so the men nodded in agreement. She would be sent to the poorhouse, a place for homeless women and children.

"Ida, you're old enough to find a job," Brother Miller said. "You're fourteen now, and you should be able to find work tending white folks' children. I'm sure someone will hire you and give you a home."

"If we sell this house, it will bring in a nice amount of money," said Brother Hall. "We can put that money along with the money you'll receive from your parents' death benefit into a trust fund. Brother Miller and I will be your guardians and look after things for you."

As Ida listened to the men talk, she grew more and more furious. During that time, children were taught by their elders to be "seen but not heard." They were told that it was bad manners to question the decisions made by adults. The men were shocked when Ida rose to her feet and interrupted the meeting.

"I've been listening to all you have had to say and I can't let you do it," Ida said calmly. "My mama and papa would turn over in their graves if they knew their children were scattered all over Holly Springs. And I can't bear the thought of Eugenia in a poorhouse. We will not be separated. If you help me find a job, I will work and take care of us."

The men stared at Ida as she walked outside and told Jim Jr. and George that it was time for bed. She knew they had been listening to the meeting and were probably worried.

"Ida," Jim Jr. whispered. "What's going to happen to us?"

"I'm going to keep you all right here at home and find work to do," Ida said. "The Masons are going to help me, and all of you will have to help too. Now go to bed. Everything's going to work out fine."

The boys hurried off to bed, and Ida returned to the meeting. The men were whispering among themselves. When they noticed Ida had come back, they stopped talking. Brother Miller rose to his feet.

"You've always done well in school, Ida," Brother Miller said. "Perhaps you can take the teaching certification examination and get a job as a school teacher. If you think you can take care of your family, then we'll do our best to help you."

Ida smiled. She hadn't thought of becoming a teacher, but she had always been a good student.

"Then it's settled," Ida said. "We have enough money to last us for a little while. We'll be all right until I can find a teaching position."

"Who will take care of the children while you're teaching?" Brother Hall asked.

"Granny Wells will come from the country if I ask her," Ida said.

"I'll send Sister Miller over to help you tomorrow," Brother Miller said. "We'll see how things go and take it from there."[3]

Ida thanked the men and got ready for bed. She hid her worries about the future from her father's friends and the other children, but she was honest about her fears in her diary.

"After being a happy, light-hearted school girl," Ida wrote, "I suddenly found myself at the head of a family."[4]

3

New Beginnings

The next morning, while Ida made breakfast, the other children crowded around Eugenia's chair. Eugenia made sure all the children's faces were clean, their teeth were brushed, and their clothes were buttoned. She combed Annie's and Lillie's hair and watched over them as they played.

"If everyone works hard, we can keep our home together," Ida said. "I'm going to try to get Grandmother to live with us."

"There's not much I can do, is there?" Eugenia said sadly.

"Yes, as much as you've always done," Ida said. "You've been the biggest help in the world. You just keep looking after Annie and Lillie. You'll be good girls and do what Genie tells you to do, won't you?" Ida asked the two little girls.

"I always do what Genie says, don't I, Genie?" Annie said. "And I make Lillie mind too."

Ida smiled at her brothers and sisters. For the first time in days she felt that things were going to get better.

Later that afternoon, Sister Miller and a few other women from the neighborhood came to help Ida. Although everyone felt that Ida would probably score high on the teacher's examination, in order to get a teaching job, she would have to look much older than fourteen. Sister Miller decided that what Ida needed was a new hairstyle.

After Sister Miller finished, she led Ida to the mirror. Ida barely recognized herself. Her long, thick black braids and pink hair bows were gone. The young lady who stared back at Ida from the mirror had her hair piled on top of her head in a neat bun.

"You know, child," Sister Miller said as she looked her over from head to toe, "young ladies wear their dresses below their shoe tops. Since you're going to play at being a young lady, you'll have to dress like one."

The women took Lizzie's dresses and cut and sewed them to fit Ida. The skirts of Ida's new dresses were so long, they trailed behind her on the floor. Ida had to practice walking so that she wouldn't trip and fall over the long skirts.[1]

That afternoon, Ida went down to the school board and took the teacher's examination. She passed and was hired to teach at a school six miles out in the country for twenty-five dollars a month. Grandmother Wells left her farm and stayed with the younger children while Ida was at work. Although she was seventy years old, Grandmother Wells was determined to help support her grandchildren. She took a job as a maid during the day, while Eugenia watched over Lillie and Annie and the boys attended school. Every evening, Grandmother Wells cleaned the house and cared for Ida's younger brothers and sisters.

From Monday through Friday, Ida lived with the Lewis family and taught in a run-down, one-room country schoolhouse. The little schoolhouse was at the intersection of two dirt roads in northern Mississippi. Ida's students sat on rough wooden benches. They had very few books or materials to write with and the walls were bare, but Ida's class was eager to learn. Ida taught everyone from young children to adults. The book most of the adults wanted to learn to read was the Bible.

As time went by, Ida became known as a very good teacher. Although Ida's students were often older than she was, they still called her "Miss Ida" and treated her with respect. Every Friday, just before Ida made the long six-mile journey home, her students showered her with gifts. Eggs, syrup, butter, and fresh vegetables were piled on the back of Ida's slow-moving mule, Ginger.

Ida's students walked with her up the road as she tried to get Ginger to trot, but she couldn't get the plump mule to move faster. At the turn in the road, the students waved good-bye to Ida and went their separate ways.

When Ida finally arrived home, Grandmother and her sisters and brothers eagerly questioned her.

"How was work, daughter?" Grandmother Wells asked. "Did everyone come to school this week?"

"What did you bring us?" her sisters and brothers asked.

"Wait, wait, one at a time!" Ida said. She showed everyone the food her students had given her and told them about her week.

"Old Ginger is getting fatter every day," Ida said as the boys led the mule away. "They keep him the whole week for me and all he has to do is eat. I told them to put him to work with their mule or he will be so fat he can't walk!"[2]

Grandmother and Ida spent all day Saturday cooking, cleaning, mending, and scrubbing. The boys shined everyone's shoes for church, and Eugenia combed Lillie's and Annie's hair. The Wells family still attended church every Sunday morning just as they had done when Jim and Lizzie were alive. On Sunday evenings, Ida would mount Ginger and ride back to the Lewises' home in the country to get ready for another week of teaching.

One evening, while Ida was away at school, Grandmother Wells suffered a stroke that paralyzed part of her body. She could no longer care for herself or the children. Ida's Aunt Belle took Grandmother Wells back to the farm to care for her. To keep her family together, Ida needed someone to watch over the children. She found a woman who had been an old friend of her mother's to stay at the house until Ida finished the school term.

Ida's Aunt Fannie, who lived in Memphis, arranged for Ida to live with her and teach at another country school in Woodstock, Tennessee. Her Aunt Belle, her mother's sister, offered to care for Eugenia, as well as Jim Jr. and George. Her brothers were old enough to be apprenticed as carpenters and were eager to learn the trade. They also helped Aunt Belle on her farm. Eugenia had become weaker and required more care and attention. Ida hated to leave her brothers and sister behind, but she felt that it was best for everyone. She took Lillie and Annie with her to Memphis to start a new life.

Although Ida's new teaching job provided her with a better salary, it was so far from Memphis that she had to ride the train to visit her family on the weekends. Every day after school, Ida studied for the Memphis Teachers' Examination. If she passed the test, she would be able to work in Memphis and would be closer to Annie and Lillie.

On May 4, 1884, Ida boarded a train to return to school in Woodstock after visiting her family. Whites and blacks paid the same price for a train ticket, but they did not receive equal accommodations or treatment. Since the end of the Civil War, many whites had found ways to take away the rights and freedoms that African-Americans had gained when slavery came to an end.

Slowly, more and more laws were being passed in the South that separated whites from blacks in public schools, restaurants, housing, and transportation. The Civil Rights Bill of 1866, which had been ratified to guarantee the rights of African-Americans, was declared unconstitutional by the United States Supreme Court in 1883. At the time Ida bought her ticket, the law stated that accommodations must be separate but equal for white and black passengers. However, white passengers rode in a clean rail car, while blacks and smokers were forced to ride in dirty, crowded cars.

When the conductor came around to collect the tickets, he refused to accept Ida's first-class pass. Ida felt that if he didn't want her ticket she wouldn't be bothered about it and continued reading her book. When the conductor finished collecting all of the tickets, he returned to Ida's seat. He told her that she would have to sit in the smoking car. Ida refused to move.

The conductor demanded that Ida move immediately. He grabbed her arm to pull her out of the seat. Although she was very small, Ida was not at all afraid of the conductor. She sank her teeth into his hand. The conductor howled in pain and left to find someone to help him remove Ida from the train. Ida braced herself by holding onto the seat in front of her and pushing her feet against the floor. If the conductor was going to try to move her, she wasn't going to make it easy for him. The conductor enlisted the help of the baggage man and another man. Together, they dragged Ida out of her seat. Ida wrote about the incident in her diary:

> [O]f course they succeeded in dragging me out. They were encouraged to do this by the attitude of the white ladies and gentlemen in the car; some of them even stood on the seats so that they could get a good view and continued applauding the conductor for his brave stand.
>
> By this time, the train had stopped at the first station. When I saw that they were determined to drag me into the smoker, which was already filled with colored people and those who were smoking, I said I would get off the train rather than go

in—which I did. Strangely, I held onto my ticket all this time, and although the sleeves of my linen duster had been torn out and I had been pretty roughly handled, I had not been hurt physically.[3]

Ida decided to fight back. She hired a lawyer to take her case to court. After her lawyer began delaying the case, and months went by, Ida discovered that the railroad had paid him to work on its side against her. Ida fired him and hired Judge Greer, who worked to bring the case to state court. The railroad approached Ida and offered her money to drop the case. Ida refused. She didn't want money—she wanted the right to be treated like any other human being. Ida's decision to fight against this injustice changed her life.

4

Iola, Princess of the Press

On December 25, 1884, the Memphis *Daily Appeal* carried this headline in bold print: **"A Darky Damsel Obtains a Verdict for Damages Against the Chesapeake and Ohio Railroad—What It Cost to Put a Colored Teacher in a Smoking Car—Verdict for $500!"**[1]

Ida had won her case and been awarded five hundred dollars, but the railroad wasn't through fighting her. The owners of the railroad appealed the case to the Tennessee Supreme Court and another judge. The owners were afraid that Ida's case would give African-Americans rights under the law that they'd lost when the Civil Rights Bill was repealed. They felt they couldn't afford to have Ida's case help bring about a more equal system under the law for whites and blacks. The railroad was also afraid others would sue.

The Tennessee Supreme Court reversed the findings of the lower court and took away both Ida's victory and her money. Because she lost the case in the Supreme Court, Ida was forced to pay two hundred dollars in damages.

By the time the case was settled, Ida had found a better-paying teaching job in Memphis, so she no longer had to travel back and forth on the train. Ida loved living in Memphis. She was twenty-five years old, and for the first time she was living in a big city. Although Ida accepted offers to teach in other states, she would always return to Memphis after a few weeks.

Unlike other young women of her time, Ida felt no real urgency to be married because she had cared for her brothers and sisters since she was a child. Ida enjoyed her life as a single young woman. For the first time, she was not responsible for anyone but herself. Her brothers, Jim Jr. and George, were both working as carpenters. Lillie and Annie had recently moved to California with their aunt Fannie. Death had taken Eugenia and Grandmother Wells within a short time of each other. Ida lived alone in various rooming houses around the city.

Ida was fond of having a male companion and had fallen in love once or twice while living in Memphis. But she hated the way that women of her time were expected to behave. "I will not begin at this late day by doing that that my soul abhors," Ida wrote in her diary, "sugaring men, weak, deceitful creatures, with flattery to retain them as escorts or to gratify a revenge."[2]

Ida was always torn between patterning herself after the quietly reserved, restrained way women of the 1800s were supposed to behave, and being true to her real self—the bold, ambitious, no-nonsense, intellectually curious, and outspoken person that she really was. This behavior was considered unladylike and masculine during the late nineteenth century.

Ida was an interesting and complicated person. She was vain and loved having her picture taken. Ida also had a passion for shopping. In her diary, she often described how she had spent too much money on a pretty dress, a hat, or pair of gloves. In her beautifully tailored clothes, she walked as if she owned the world.

Ida had many interests, including attending the large African-American churches in Memphis to hear the sermons; going horseback riding; watching baseball games; attending concerts and plays; participating in lively conversations; playing checkers and Parcheesi; and traveling. She attended summer sessions at Fisk University in Nashville, Tennessee, and enjoyed learning and debating about every aspect of a topic.

Ida also loved to read. She wrote in her diary that "I had formed my ideals on the best of [Charles] Dickens's stories, Louisa May Alcott's, Mrs. A. D. T. Whitney's and Charlotte Brontë's books, and Oliver Optic's stories for boys. I had read the Bible and Shakespeare through, but I had never read a Negro book or anything about Negroes."[3] Her detailed diary and journal entries are evidence that she enjoyed writing as well.

Ida was a member of a literary club that met every Friday afternoon. The young men and women, most of whom were teachers, enjoyed quoting from their favorite books, making speeches, reading essays they had written, and listening to music. At the end of each meeting, they read aloud from a newspaper called the *Evening Star*. Ida described the paper as "a spicy journal." Owned and written by

African-Americans, it offered its readers thought-provoking news and opinions. When the editor of the *Evening Star* moved to Washington, D.C., Ida was chosen to take his place. "I tried to make my offering as acceptable as his had been," Ida wrote in her diary, "and before long I found that I liked the work."[4] Ida enjoyed writing items for the paper and reading them aloud at the Friday afternoon meetings.

Other newspapers began reprinting Ida's articles, and she received an offer to write for a paper published by the Baptist church called *The Living Way*. Ida's first article for *The Living Way* was a detailed account of her court case against the railroad. African-American newspapers around the United States reprinted the article.

Ida believed that her articles should tell a reader the truth in a simple, no-nonsense way. She signed her work "Iola," and African-American newspapers in other states regularly reprinted her pieces and asked her to write new articles for them. She was elected secretary of the Colored Press Association in 1889. The National Press Association called Ida "the princess of the press."

Although she was still working as a teacher, writing became more and more appealing to Ida. "I had made a reputation in school for thoroughness and discipline in the primary grades," Ida noted in her diary, "[but] I was never promoted above the fourth grade in all my years as a teacher. The confinement and monotony of the primary work began to grow distasteful. The correspondence I had built up in newspaper work gave me an outlet through which to express the real 'me,' and I enjoyed my work to the utmost."[5]

When Ida was twenty-seven years old, she was offered the opportunity to write for the *Memphis Free Speech and Headlight*, which was owned by J. L. Fleming and Reverend Taylor Nightingale, pastor of one of the largest African-American churches in town. "I refused to come in except as equal with themselves, and I bought a one-third interest," Ida wrote. "I was editor, Mr. Fleming was business manager, and Rev. Nightingale was sales manager."[6]

Ida continued teaching during the day to pay for the newspaper and to support herself. She spent her nights and weekends at the newspaper. She decided that something needed to be done to improve the poor condition of the school buildings for African-

Americans and the outdated books and materials black children had to use at school. She wrote an article about the schools that also criticized the qualifications of some of the African-American teachers.

"Needless to say," Ida wrote later, "that article created a sensation and much comment." Because of what she had written, Ida lost her teaching position. "But I thought it was right to strike a blow against a glaring evil and I did not regret it."[7]

Ida was determined to make a living as a writer. She began traveling around the country to introduce people to her newspaper and to urge them to subscribe. "In nine months," Ida wrote, "I had an income as nearly as large as I had received teaching and felt sure that I had found my vocation. I was very proud of my success because up to that time very few of our newspapers had made any money."[8]

Ida purchased Reverend Nightingale's share of the paper and became co-owner with J. L. Fleming. Then she began printing the newspaper on pink paper so that it stood out from other newspapers.

In March 1892, Ida sadly noted in her diary that "while I was thus carrying on the work of my newspaper, happy in the thought that our influence was helpful and I was doing the work I loved and had proved I could make a living out of it, there came the lynching in Memphis which changed the whole course of my life."[9]

A lynching occurs when an angry mob kills a person without due process of law. Since the beginning of the American slave trade in the eighteenth century, hundreds of African-American men, women, and children had been lynched. Although Ida knew that lynchings happened fairly often in the South, she had felt that the person who was lynched had done something wrong to deserve such a horrible punishment. The incident that became known as "the lynching at the Curve" affected her deeply and changed her views about lynching forever.

Thomas Moss and his wife, Betty, were two of Ida's closest friends. She was godmother to their daughter, Maurine. Thomas was a mail carrier who visited Ida's newspaper offices every day with letters and the latest news around town. Moss, along with Calvin McDowell and Henry Stewart, owned a business they called the People's

Ida with her friend Betty Moss, the widow of Thomas Moss, and Betty's children, Thomas Jr. and Maurine. Ida was Maurine's godmother. Thomas Moss was lynched by a mob in 1892.

Grocery Company in an area of Memphis known as "the Curve," because the streetcar tracks curved sharply at that point.

For a long time, a white grocery store had received most of the business in that area. When Thomas Moss and his partners opened their store, they began attracting many of the shoppers. Their business blossomed and their success made the other storekeeper jealous and angry. An argument at the Curve between a group of children, some white and some black, erupted into threats to "clean out the People's Grocery Company."

Moss and his partners consulted a lawyer who told them that they would not receive police protection because they were outside of the city limits. He advised them to arm themselves and protect their property. That night, March 5, 1892, around ten o'clock, three white men broke into the back of the People's Grocery Company and were shot and wounded.

The white-owned newspapers in Memphis ran several untrue stories claiming that the men who broke into the store were officers of the law, and that they were "hunting up criminals whom they had been told were harbored in the People's Grocery Company . . . a resort of thieves and thugs."[10]

The Memphis police used the incident as an excuse to raid the homes of more than one hundred African-American men and arrest and jail them on charges of "suspicion." Some white men were allowed inside the jail to point out the owners of the People's Grocery Company. Fearing trouble, several black men in Memphis armed themselves and stood outside the jail to prevent any lynchings. After a couple of days, the men believed that the tension had eased and the crisis had passed, so they stopped standing guard at the jail.

That very night, the guards let a mob of white men into the jail. They yanked Thomas Moss, Calvin McDowell, and Henry Stewart out of their cells and took them outside the city limits to Cubbins Brick Yard. An eyewitness account said that Thomas Moss "begged for his life for the sake of his wife and child and his unborn baby." When asked if he had any last words, Moss said "tell my people to go West—there is no justice for them here."[11]

It was an unwritten rule that to kill a black person in America was not a crime. White mob rule prevailed over the letter of the law.

The news of the lynching shocked African-Americans in Memphis. They gathered together at the grocery store to talk quietly and mourn the deaths of their friends.

By the time Ida returned to town from her trip to Mississippi, her dear friend Thomas Moss had already been buried. She wanted to honor his life and protest his death, so she wrote this article, which appeared on the front page of the *Memphis Free Speech and Headlight*:

> The city of Memphis has demonstrated that neither character nor standing avails the Negro if he dares to protect himself against the white man or become his rival. There is nothing we can do about the lynching now, as we are out-numbered and without arms. The white mob could help itself to ammunition without pay, but the order is rigidly enforced against the selling of guns to Negroes. There is therefore only one thing left that we can do: save our money and leave a town which will neither protect our lives and property, nor give us a fair trial in the courts, but takes us out and murders us in cold blood when accused by white persons.[13]

During Ida's lifetime, African-Americans very seldom spoke out so forcefully. It was also unusual for a woman to say the things that Ida said. Ida's strongly worded article was a brave statement.

5

Crusade for Justice

African-Americans began leaving Memphis by the hundreds. Those who stayed refused to support businesses owned by whites. Local companies such as clothing and furniture and grocery stores depended on African-Americans for their business and lost thousands of dollars. The City Railway Company asked Ida to assure her readers that they would be treated courteously on the streetcars. Ida refused, writing in her diary that "she had never walked so much in her life. . . . Every time word came of people leaving Memphis, we who were left behind rejoiced. Oklahoma was about to be opened up, and scores sold or gave away property, shook Memphis dust off their feet, and went out West as Tom Moss had said for us to do."[1]

Several white newspapers began printing horrible stories about life in Oklahoma to discourage African-Americans from moving there. The papers said that those who left for Oklahoma faced starvation and hostile Native Americans. Ida decided to report on the true conditions in the West and traveled to Guthrie, Oklahoma, Oklahoma City, and other settlements in the territory. Her favorable articles encouraged even more people to move west, including African-Americans who lived in Arkansas, Mississippi, and sections of Tennessee. Although African-Americans still faced racism, the West gave them an opportunity to build their own communities.

Ida also began investigating every lynching that she heard of or read about. She wrote that the deaths of Thomas Moss, Calvin McDowell, and Henry Stewart had "opened my eyes to what lynching really was. An excuse to get rid of Negroes who were acquiring wealth and property and thus keep the race terrorized."[2]

Ida decided that she had to expose lynching to the world and help bring it to an end. She visited Tunica County and Natchez, Mississippi, the sites of two lynchings, to collect the facts and take sworn statements from eyewitnesses. She corresponded with witnesses in other towns where lynchings had occurred. Ida used accounts from white newspapers and let the words of white Southerners speak for themselves to establish the facts about lynching and mob violence. This prevented anyone from saying her accounts were distorted or inaccurate. Ida knew how powerful the written word was.

In 1892, she turned her notes and correspondence into her first published pamphlet about lynching, titled *Southern Horrors*. Ida published two other pamphlets about lynching and mob violence, *A Red Record: Tabulated Statistics and Alleged Causes of Lynching in the United States, 1892, 1893, and 1894*, and *Mob Rule in New Orleans*, an account of race riots in New Orleans in 1900. She often used pamphlets to protest against injustice. In 1893, she published a little book called *The Reason Why the Colored American is not in the World's Columbian Exposition* to protest the exclusion of African-Americans from the 1893 World's Fair in Chicago.

Ida was invited to travel to the African Methodist Episcopal General Conference in Philadelphia, and to go to New York to visit T. Thomas Fortune and Jerome B. Peterson, owners of the *New York Age*, a widely circulated African-American newspaper that often reprinted Ida's articles. Before leaving Memphis, Ida wrote an editorial to be published in the *Memphis Free Speech*.

The editorial angered many white citizens in Memphis. They felt Ida's article was insulting to white women. They destroyed the offices, furniture, and presses of the *Memphis Free Speech*. Ida's business partner, J. L. Fleming, received a warning from a leading citizen of Memphis and barely escaped being lynched himself. He traveled west, finally settling in Kansas. Ida's friends sent letters informing her that if she ever returned to Memphis she would be killed on sight. The trains and her house were being watched. Ida would never be able to go home to Memphis again.

Ida wrote in her diary:

> I accepted their advice and took a position on the *New York Age* and continued my fight against lynching and lynchers. They had destroyed my paper, in which every dollar I had in the world was invested. They had made me an exile and threatened my life for hinting at the truth. I felt I owed it to myself and my race to tell the whole truth.[4]

Ida received a salary and one-fourth ownership of the *New York Age*. She wrote a full account of her lynching investigations and the destruction of her presses. The *New York Age* published her article on June 7, 1892, in a seven-column spread. Ida named names and cited dates and places for many of the lynchings. It was a bold and shocking article, unlike any other during that time. Ten thousand copies of the paper were printed and distributed around the country and throughout the South. One thousand copies were sold in Memphis alone.

Ida began receiving requests from around the country to give speeches about the horrors of lynching. Her first appearance was before a group of African-American women in New York. After Ida's moving speech, the women banded together to do something about lynching and organized one of the first clubs among African-American women in New York.

American women did not have the right to vote, but they began to realize the power they possessed as an organized group to fight against injustices in American society. The club movement spread among women of all races, and Ida helped to form a few of the African-American organizations. Several groups began calling themselves Ida B. Wells Clubs and are still in existence today. Ida's speeches, pamphlets, and newspaper articles helped other women realize that they had the intelligence, the ability, and the obligation to improve life for their families and communities.

Ms. Catherine Impey, a young woman from Somerset,

Ida B. Wells, 1893

England, heard Ida speak and requested that she visit England, Scotland, and Wales to give speeches about lynching. Ida traveled to Great Britain twice, once in 1893 and a second time in 1894. She stayed several months each time, speaking to hundreds of people about injustice in America. Great Britain was a new experience for Ida. For the first time she received courteous and respectful treatment from white people and their support in her cause to stop lynching. She described her travels in several letters to the *New York Age*. These articles also appeared in other African-American newspapers.

Ida's travels left her very tired. When she returned to America, she decided to make her home in Chicago. There was a growing club movement in that city, and Ida had met a tall, handsome, young widower with two young boys named Ferdinand Lee Barnett. He was an attorney and founder of the city's first African-American newspaper, the *Chicago Conservator*. Ferdinand and Ida were both strong-willed, outspoken, and passionate about the cause of equal rights for African-Americans. Although Ida was usually serious, stubborn, and had few close friends because of her blunt and forceful opinions, Ferdinand was just the opposite. He loved to tease, entertain friends, and tell jokes.

Ferdinand and Ida were married on June 27, 1895. Ida was thirty-three years old. Hundreds of people crowded into the chapel and lined the streets to catch a glimpse of the wedding party.

Many people were happy for Ida, but others, like women's rights activist Susan B. Anthony,

Ferdinand L. Barnett Sr., Ida's husband

believed her marriage was a mistake and criticized her. Few women during the 1800s had the freedom and power that Ida possessed to make a difference in the lives of women.

Ferdinand realized the importance of Ida's crusade against lynching and recognized her unique talents as a writer and speaker. He wanted her to continue with her work and made it possible for her to do so. He sold Ida his share in *The Chicago Conservator*. She bought the interest of the other partners as well and, for the first time, had full ownership of her own newspaper. In addition, he did not object to her keeping her own name and simply adding Barnett, a bold action for married women to take at that time.

Ida and Ferdinand became the parents of four children: Charles, Herman, Ida Jr., and Alfreda. Ida pursued the task of being a mother with the same zeal she had devoted to her professional life. "I found that motherhood was a profession by itself, just like schoolteaching and lecturing," she wrote in her diary, "and that once one was launched on such a career, she owed it to herself to become as expert as possible in the practice of her profession."[5] She gave up the paper after Herman's birth in 1897 and did not work outside of the home again until Alfreda was eight years old, although she continued to speak out against injustice and attended meetings in other states, taking her baby along with her.

6

The Price of Liberty

Ida once said that "the price of liberty is eternal vigilance."[1] She knew that in order to keep the small gains African-Americans had made in their struggle for equal rights, she would have to continue to speak, write, and petition for justice.

Ida was constantly busy reading, writing, and speaking. She continued her duties as president of the Chicago Ida B. Wells Club and her speaking engagements, often bringing her baby, Alfreda, along with her. She was one of the founding members of the National Afro-American Council, the organization that later became the National Association for the Advancement of Colored People (NAACP), and petitioned both Presidents William McKinley and Woodrow Wilson to sign laws that guaranteed just treatment for African-Americans.

Ida's family fully supported her work against injustice. After a lynching in Cairo, Illinois, her husband urged Ida to go investigate. Ida wrote about the incident in her diary:

> It was not very convenient for me to be leaving home at that time, and for once, I was quite willing to let them [African-American men] attend to the job. . . . I picked up my baby and took her upstairs to bed. As usual I not only sang her to sleep but put myself to sleep lying there beside her. I was awakened by my oldest child [Charles] who said, "Mother, Pa says it is time to go." "Go where?" I said. "To take the train to Cairo. . . . Mother, if you don't go nobody else will." The next morning all four of my children accompanied my husband and me to the station and saw me start on the journey.[2]

While Ida traveled, Ferdinand often stayed behind to tend to his successful law practice and care for the children. He cooked dinner every night because he enjoyed it and Ida didn't like to, although she did enjoy baking bread.

In 1919, the Barnetts moved to a beautiful home with eight rooms, a ballroom, and a full basement. The Barnetts loved company and often entertained distinguished guests, such as civil rights leader A. Philip Randolph and historian Carter G. Woodson, along with those who were poor, unknown, and less fortunate. The entire family enjoyed playing whist, a card game, and listening to ragtime and opera records on their Victrola. Ida loved the theater and had wanted to become an actress when she was younger, something that was frowned upon by society during her time. She often took her children to the Avenue Theater to see performances by Bert Williams, the Ziegfeld Follies, and actor Abby Mitchell.

Ida B. Wells and her four children in 1909: Charles, age fourteen; Herman, age twelve; Ida Jr., age eight; and Alfreda, age five

Although Ida had very little contact with her brothers, Jim Jr. and George, she remained close to her sisters. Lillie was married and lived in California. Annie lived in Chicago, where she owned a successful newspaper called *The Searchlight*. The sisters visited often.

Ida continued to get involved in politics and to assist those who needed her help. In 1913, the Barnetts started the Negro Fellowship League in Chicago to improve the plight of African-Americans through better housing, financial assistance, employment counseling, and recreation. For ten years, they ran the league with little financial support from anyone other than themselves. During three of those years, Ida worked as a probation officer. She set up an office in the Negro Fellowship League building to counsel those who were in trouble with the law.

In 1914, Ida became more active in securing women's right to vote and to use the power of the ballot. Suffragettes, as women who wanted to vote were called, were often accused of "trying to take the place of men and wear trousers," said Ida.[3] Very few African-American women in Chicago had been involved in the suffrage movement before Ida started the Alpha Suffrage Club.

The Barnett family in 1917: **Standing:** *Hulette D. Barnett (wife of Albert G. Barnett, Ferdinand's son by his first wife, Margaret Graham Barnett); Herman Kohlsaat Barnett; Ferdinand L. Barnett Jr. (his other son from his first marriage); Ida Jr.; Charles; Alfreda; and Albert G. Barnett*
Seated: *Ferdinand L. Barnett Sr.; Beatrice Barnett and Audrey Barnett (Albert's daughters); Ida B. Wells-Barnett*
Foreground: *Hulette E. Barnett and Florence B. Barnett (Albert's daughters)*

Ida B. Wells-Barnett, 1920

Ida also continued to investigate lynchings, mob violence, and injustice. She played an active part in the committee inquiry into the East Saint Louis riot in 1918, which left 150 people dead and a million dollars' worth of property destroyed.

Ida believed that this disturbance was only the beginning of the city's troubles. In a letter to the *Chicago Tribune*, Ida urged Chicago city leaders to "set the wheels of justice in motion before it was too late." The city took no action, and one of the bloodiest race riots in history erupted shortly afterward.

Ida also arranged small protests of her own. She'd heard that a local department store refused to wait on African-American customers. She visited the store to see if the reports were true. Sure enough, no one would wait on her. Finally she took a pair of men's underwear, draped them over her arm, and walked toward the door. She was assisted immediately. She could never tell the story without laughing.

In 1920, Ida was hospitalized for gall bladder surgery. She spent most all of the following year recovering from the surgery, but as soon as she was able to, Ida became active again in Chicago politics.

Because she was one of the founders of the women's club movement in her city, Ida was very disappointed when she was defeated by educator Mary McLeod Bethune for the presidency of the National Association of Colored Women in 1924. In 1930, Ida lost an election to become an Illinois state senator, but paved the way for other women to pursue a career in politics.

As Ida grew older, she began to feel that her struggles for equality and fairness were being ignored in the history books. After attending a reading at the local Negro History Club in 1928, Ida was disappointed to find no mention about her work as an activist in Carter G. Woodson's book *Negro Makers of History*. Ida decided it was time to write her autobiography and began working on the story of her life in diary form.

"I did more serious thinking from a personal point of view than ever before in my life," Ida wrote. "All at once the realization came to me that I had nothing to show for all those years of toil and labor."[4]

After a brief illness, Ida died suddenly of uremic poisoning, the result of a kidney disease that poisoned her blood, on March 25, 1931, before completing her book. She was sixty-eight years old. She left behind two diaries, one of which became *Crusade for Justice: The Autobiography of Ida B. Wells*, which details Ida's struggles and devotion to the cause of civil rights. Her other diary is titled *The Memphis Diary of Ida B. Wells: An Intimate Portrait of the Activist as a Young Woman*, and chronicles Ida's years as a young school teacher in Memphis.

After her death, Ida received many of the honors she had wished for during her life. The Ida B. Wells Homes, a federal housing project, was constructed on what is now Martin Luther King Boulevard in Chicago, across from the site of Ida's home, which has been declared a historical landmark. In 1950, the city of Chicago named Ida one of the twenty-five outstanding women in the city's history. On the one hundred and twenty-fifth anniversary of her birth, the Tennessee Historical Commission and the Memphis Community Relations Council placed a historical marker at the site of her *Memphis Free Speech* offices.

The United States Postal Service honored Ida with a postage stamp during Black History Month in 1990. She is also included in several biographical collections about famous women. The details of Ida B. Wells's life and her wonderful achievements are now an important part of modern history books.

Ida left a legacy of public service for the good of all people. She demonstrated the power of the written word for women and men of all races. Her courage to seek as well as speak the truth and her unwavering fight for justice, often as a lone warrior, helped to change the course of American history.

Chronology

1862	Born in Holly Springs, Mississippi, on July 16.
1866	Rust College (formerly Shaw University), a high school and industrial school for newly freed slaves, is established. Ida attended this school later in her life.
1876	Ida's mother, father, and baby brother die of yellow fever. Ida becomes the head of her family.
1884	Ida is forced off the train on the Memphis-to-Woodstock line. She sues the railroad company, and the court rules in her favor, awarding her five hundred dollars.
1887	The Tennessee Supreme Court reverses the lower court's ruling, and Ida is forced to pay court costs. Ida writes about the case for *The Living Way*, a religious weekly.
1889	Ida buys part of the *Memphis Free Speech and Headlight* and becomes secretary of the Colored Press Association.
1891	The Memphis Board of Education fires Ida because of a critical article she wrote about the schools for African-American children and the conduct of some of their teachers.
1892	Thomas Moss, Calvin McDowell, and Henry Stewart, owners of the People's Grocery Company, are lynched. The article that Ida writes about the incident angers many white townspeople. Mobs destroy her presses and threaten her life. Ida is forced to move to the North.
1893	Ida begins her first speaking tour throughout England, Scotland, and Wales to expose the injustice of lynching.
1895	Ferdinand L. Barnett and Ida B. Wells are married on June 27.
1909	The NAACP is formed. Ida serves on the executive committee.
1913	The Barnetts establish the Negro Fellowship League to assist African-Americans in Chicago. Ida starts the Alpha Suffrage Club to secure women's right to vote, and becomes a probation officer.

1920   Ida undergoes surgery to remove her gall bladder and is slow
        to recover.

1924   Mary McLeod Bethune defeats Ida for president of the National
        Association of Colored Women.

1930   Ida loses an election to become a state senator in Illinois.

1931   Ida dies on March 25, after a brief illness.

Endnotes

Chapter 1

1. Alfreda M. Duster, ed., *Crusade for Justice: The Autobiography of Ida B. Wells* (Chicago: University of Chicago Press, 1970, 1972), p. 10.

2. Ibid., p. 15.

3. Ibid., p. 8.

4. Ibid., p. 9.

5. Ibid., p. 11.

6. Ibid.

7. Ibid., p. 12.

Chapter 2

1. Alfreda M. Duster, untitled and unpublished manuscript, *Biography of Ida B. Wells*, p. 5.

2. Ibid., p. 6.

3. Ibid., chapter 2, pp. 1–3.

4. Alfreda M. Duster, ed., *Crusade for Justice: The Autobiography of Ida B. Wells* (Chicago: University of Chicago Press, 1970, 1972), p. 16.

Chapter 3

1. Alfreda M. Duster, untitled and unpublished manuscript, p. 7.

2. Ibid., chapter 3-1, p. 2.

3. Alfreda M. Duster, ed., *Crusade for Justice: The Autobiography of Ida B. Wells* (Chicago: University of Chicago Press, 1970, 1972), p. 19.

Chapter 4

1. Alfreda M. Duster, ed., *Crusade for Justice: The Autobiography of Ida B. Wells* (Chicago: University of Chicago Press, 1970, 1972), p. 19.

2. Miriam DeCosta-Willis, ed., *The Memphis Diary of Ida B. Wells: An Intimate Portrait of the Activist as a Young Woman* (Boston: Beacon Press, 1995), p. 37.

3. Ibid., pp. 21–22.

4. Ibid., p. 23.

5. Ibid., p. 31.

6. Ibid., p. 35.

7. Ibid., p. 36.

8. Ibid., p. 39.

9. Ibid., p. 47.

10. Ibid., p. 49.

11. Ibid., pp. 50–51.

13. Ibid., p. 52.

Chapter 5

1. Miriam DeCosta-Willis, ed., *The Memphis Diary of Ida B. Wells: An Intimate Portrait of the Activist as a Young Woman* (Boston: Beacon Press, 1995), p. 55.

2. Ibid., p. 64.

4. Ibid., pp. 62–63.

5. Ibid., pp. 250–51.

Chapter 6

1. Miriam DeCosta-Willis, ed., *The Memphis Diary of Ida B. Wells: An Intimate Portrait of the Activist as a Young Woman* (Boston: Beacon Press, 1995), p. 415.

2. Ibid., pp. 311–12.

3. Ibid., p. 346.

4. Ibid., p. 414.

IN MY CORNER

Friendly, Flashy, Fancy Fonts

By BERNARD MOLLY
Obsidian Journal Columnist

You may have noticed while reading this issue of the *Obsidian Journal* that something appears a bit . . . different. Beginning today, the *Journal* is printing all articles using the Utopia font. You may ask: Why the change? What forces lead a newspaper or a magazine or an advertiser to choose one font over another?

We felt it was time for a change here at the "old" *Journal*. We wanted to freshen up our look to keep up with the changing times. We talked to consultants, polled our readers, and looked at hundreds of ideas for fonts and page layouts before making our choice. We wanted type that was readable but still decorative. Utopia beat out all others.

The creation of fonts dates back all the way to Johannes Gutenberg and his invention of the printing press in the early 1400s. Metal-and-machine processes at that time (and for a long time after) were not cheap, nor were they quick or easy. As recently as the 1950s, designers created fonts by carving letters into lead as slowly as one letter per day.

Today, the digital age has made font creation almost as easy as the click of a mouse. There are tens of thousands of typefaces available for all sorts of fees. The companies that create these fonts, both large corporations and smaller firms, sell the fonts for as little as fifty dollars. Digital technology even allows people to create their own personalized fonts.

Why the font rage? In many ways, the typeface you choose for your school or business report or to build a Web site reflects your personality. Are you elegant, rounded, and cursive, or strong, bold, and sans serif? (Serifs are the little curves and lines on the edges of letter strokes, of which Utopia has many.) And this trend of signature fonts has spilled into the world of celebrities. Both singer/actress Beyoncé Knowles and model Kate Moss use unique fonts for their names that help convey to the world their image and character.

Want to find a font that has another layer of familiarity? The Internet contains site upon site selling fonts that resemble typefaces used for the opening credits of TV shows such as *Family Guy* or *Jeopardy!* Or you might find a font with a more subtle meaning. The font P22 Cézanne was created based on the handwriting of the famous French Impressionist painter, Paul Cézanne.

And one more point about that subtle meaning. One Canadian student asked his college professors which typeface they liked most among those he used for his term papers and found the winner to be the Georgia font. So the next time you're tempted to use an old stand-by like Helvetica or Times New Roman, go crazy and consider that ever-growing world of typefaces. Let your personality be your guide.

We at the *Journal* hope you like our decision and our new "face." ∎

Cézanne

PAUL CÉZANNE'S SIGNATURE, the inspiration for the font P22 Cézanne

g

UTOPIA BOLD

Soib

DISTINCTIVE UTOPIA TRAITS

Extension Activity

Connecting with a Character: Ferdinand Lee Barnett supported Ida B. Wells-Barnett in many ways. (a) Describe Ferdinand, and discuss two ways he had an impact on Ida's life. (b) Think of someone who has had an impact in this way on your life. Describe this person and two ways this person has affected you. (c) Write a summary of your paper.

Paper Requirements: Paper must begin with a title page that lists the paper's title, your name, and the date. Paper must be two or three pages long (not including the title page).

Also By The Author

If you enjoyed *Princess of the Press,* you may enjoy these other books by Angela Shelf Medearis:

- *Dare to Dream: Coretta Scott King and the Civil Rights Movement* (nonfiction; a biography that chronicles the life of a courageous woman)
- *Little Louis and the Jazz Band: The Story of Louis "Satchmo" Armstrong* (nonfiction; a narrative about Armstrong's youth and rise to fame)
- *Seven Spools of Thread: A Kwanzaa Story* (fiction; uses a folktale to tell the story of Kwanzaa; contains holiday crafts and recipes)
- *Too Much Talk: A West African Folktale* (fiction; a folktale attributed to Ghana)

Related Topics

If you enjoyed the topics discussed in *Princess of the Press,* you may enjoy these other books that explore similar topics:

- *Extraordinary Women Journalists* by Claire Price-Groff (nonfiction; collection of biographies of women in journalism)
- *From Gutenberg to Open Type: An Illustrated History of Type from the Earliest Letterforms to the Latest Digital Fonts* by Robin Dodd (nonfiction; illustrated history of printing)
- *Johannes Gutenberg and the Printing Press* by Diana Childress (nonfiction; account of Gutenberg and the invention that propelled Europe into its modern era)
- *Up Close: Oprah Winfrey* by Ilene Cooper (nonfiction; about another well-known woman in the media, covering Winfrey's childhood and rise to fame)

Phineas Gage

A Gruesome but True Story About Brain Science

By John Fleischman

"Horrible Accident" in Vermont

The most unlucky/lucky moment in the life of Phineas Gage is only a minute or two away. It's almost four-thirty in the afternoon on September 13, 1848. Phineas is the foreman of a track construction gang that is in the process of blasting a railroad right-of-way through granite bedrock near the small town of Cavendish, Vermont. Phineas is twenty-six years old, unmarried, and five feet, six inches tall, short for our time but about average for his. He is good with his hands and good with his men, "possessing an iron will as well as an iron frame," according to his doctor. In a moment, Phineas will have a horrible accident.

It will kill him, but it will take another eleven years, eight months, and eight days to do so. In the short run, Phineas will make a full recovery, or so it will seem to those who didn't know him before. Old friends and family will know the truth. Phineas will never be his old self again. His "character" will change. The ways in which he deals with others, conducts himself, and makes plans will all change. Long after the accident, his doctor will sum up his case for a medical journal. "Gage," his doctor will write, "was no longer Gage." Phineas Gage's accident will make him world famous, but fame will do him little good. Yet for many others—psychologists, medical researchers, doctors, and especially those who suffer brain injuries—Phineas Gage will become someone worth knowing.

That's why we know so much about Phineas. It's been 150 years since his accident, yet we are still learning more about him. There's also a lot about Phineas we don't know and probably never will. The biggest question is the simplest one and the hardest to answer: Was Phineas lucky or unlucky? Once you hear his story, you can decide for yourself. But right now, Phineas is working on the railroad and his time has nearly come.

Building a railroad in 1848 is muscle work. There are no bulldozers or power shovels to open a way through Vermont's Green Mountains for the Rutland & Burlington Railroad. Phineas's men work with picks, shovels, and rock drills. Phineas's special skill is blasting. With well-placed charges of black gunpowder, he shatters rock. To set those

charges, he carries the special tool of the blasting trade, his "tamping iron." Some people confuse a tamping iron with a crowbar, but they are different tools for different jobs. A crowbar is for lifting up or prying apart something heavy. A tamping iron is for the delicate job of setting explosives. Phineas had his tamping iron made to order by a neighborhood blacksmith. It's a tapering iron rod that is three feet, seven inches long and weighs thirteen and a half pounds. It looks like an iron spear. At the base, it's fat and round, an inch and three quarters in diameter. The fat end is for tamping—packing down—loose powder. The other end comes to a sharp, narrow point and is for poking holes through the gunpowder to set the fuse. Phineas's tamping iron is very smooth to the touch, smooth from the blacksmith's forge as well as from constant use.

His task is to blast the solid rock into pieces small enough for his crew to dig loose with hand tools and haul away in ox carts. The first step is to drill a hole in the bedrock at exactly the right angle and depth, or the explosion will be wasted. All day, Phineas must keep an eye on his drillers to make sure they stay ahead. All day, Phineas must keep an eye on his diggers to make sure they keep up. All the time between, Phineas and his assistant are working with touchy explosives.

They follow a strict routine. His assistant "charges" each new hole by filling the bottom with coarse-grained gunpowder. Phineas uses the narrow end of his iron to carefully press the ropelike fuse down into the powder. The assistant then fills up the rest of the hole with loose sand to act as a plug. Phineas will tamp the sand tight to bottle up the explosion, channeling the blast downward into the rock to shatter it. While his assistant is pouring the sand, Phineas flips his tamping iron around from the pointy end to the round end for tamping. Black powder is ticklish stuff. When it's damp, nothing will set it off. When it's too dry or mixed in the wrong formula, almost anything can set it off, without warning. But Phineas and his assistant have done this a thousand times—pour the powder, set the fuse, pour the sand, tamp the sand plug, shout a warning, light the fuse, and run like mad.

This is the face of the man with a hole in his head. It's a plaster life mask of Phineas Gage made in Boston after his accident, and it shows exactly what the "recovered" Phineas looked like a year after his accident. He was twenty-seven. Notice the big scar on his forehead. To see what lies beneath the scar, compare this to the picture of his skull on page 188.

But something goes wrong this time. The sand is never poured down the hole; the black powder and fuse sit exposed at the bottom. Does his assistant forget, or does Phineas forget to look? Witnesses disagree. A few yards behind Phineas, a group of his men are using a hand-cranked derrick crane to hoist a large piece of rock. Some of the men remember seeing Phineas standing over the blast hole, leaning lightly on the tamping iron. Others say Phineas was sitting on a rock ledge above the hole, holding the iron loosely between his knees.

There is no argument about what happens next. Something or someone distracts Phineas. Does he hear his name called? Does he spot someone goofing off? Whatever the reason, Phineas turns his head to glance over his right shoulder. The fat end of his tamping iron slips down into the hole and strikes the granite. A spark flies onto the exposed blasting powder. Blam! The drill hole acts as a gun barrel. Instead of a bullet, it fires Phineas's rod straight upward. The iron shrieks through the air and comes down with a loud clang about thirty feet away.

This is what happens. Imagine you are inside Phineas's head, watching in extreme slow motion: See the pointy end of the rod enter under his left cheekbone, pass behind his left eye, through the front of his brain, and out the middle of his forehead just above the hairline. It takes a fraction of a fraction of a second for the iron rod to pass from cheekbone to forehead, through and through.

Amazingly, Phineas is still alive. The iron throws him flat on his back, but as his men come running through the gunpowder smoke, he sits up. A minute later, he speaks. Blood is pouring down his face from his forehead, but Phineas is talking about the explosion. His men insist on carrying him to an ox cart for the short ride into town. They gently lift him into the back of the cart so he can sit up with his legs out before him on the floor. An Irish workman grabs a horse and races ahead for the doctor while the ox cart ambulance rumbles slowly down the half-mile to Cavendish. Phineas's excited men crowd alongside, walking next to their injured boss. Still acting as a foreman, Phineas calls out for his time book and makes an entry as he rolls toward town.

> Lucky or unlucky, the sharp angle of the tamping iron made all the difference to Phineas. It entered just under his left cheekbone, passed behind his left eyeball, and continued on upward through his frontal lobes. It exited his forehead between the two hemispheres of the cortex. The iron's passage left him alive and conscious but forever changed.

Something terrible has happened, yet Phineas gets down from the cart without help. He climbs the steps of the Cavendish hotel, where he has been living, and takes a seat on the porch beside his landlord, Joseph Adams. A few minutes earlier, Adams had seen the Irishman ride past shouting for Dr. Harlow, the town physician. Dr. Harlow was not to be found, so the rider was sent on to the next village to

Phineas Gage

fetch Dr. Williams. Now Phineas takes a neighborly seat on the porch and tells his landlord what happened to him.

That's how Dr. Edward Williams finds Phineas nearly thirty minutes after the accident. Dr. Williams pulls up in his buggy at the hotel porch, and there is Phineas, talking away. Friends, workmates, and the curious crowd around as Dr. Williams climbs down from his carriage. "Well, here's work enough for you, Doctor," Phineas says to him quite cheerfully.

Dr. Williams examines Phineas's head. He can't believe that this man is still alive. His skull is cracked open, as if something has popped out from the inside. Accident victims are often too shaken to know what happened, so Dr. Williams turns to Phineas's workmen for the story, but Phineas insists on speaking for himself. He tells Dr. Williams that the iron went right through his head.

Dr. Williams does not believe him. "I thought he was deceived," Dr. Williams writes in his notes. "I asked him where the bar entered, and he pointed to the wound on his cheek, which I had not before discovered. This was a slit running from the angle of the jaw forward about one and a half inch. It was very much stretched laterally, and was discolored by powder and iron rust, at least appeared

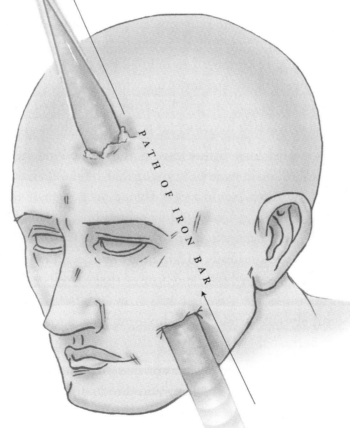

PATH OF IRON BAR

so. Mr. Gage persisted in saying that the bar went through his head. An Irishman standing by said, 'Sure it was so, sir, for the bar is lying in the road below, all blood and brains.'"

It's now an hour after the accident. The town's regular physician, Dr. John Martyn Harlow, finally arrives at the hotel. The two doctors confer, but Dr. Harlow takes over the case. Phineas is a gruesome sight. Bleeding freely from his forehead and inside his mouth, Phineas looks to Dr. Harlow like a wounded man just carried in from a battlefield. Yet Phineas is alert, uncomplaining, and still telling anyone who'll listen about the accident. Dr. Harlow wants Phineas to come in off the porch so he can treat his wound. Phineas gets up and, leaning only lightly on Dr. Harlow's arm, climbs up a long flight of stairs to his room. He lies down on his own bed so Dr. Harlow can shave his head and examine the wound more closely. What the doctor sees is terrible. Something has erupted through the top of Phineas's head, shattering the skull in its path and opening the brain to plain sight.

Dr. Harlow does what he can. He cleans the skin around the hole, extracts the small fragments of bone, and gently presses the larger pieces of skull back in place. He looks inside Phineas's mouth. He can see the hole where the iron passed upward through the roof of his mouth. Dr. Harlow decides to leave the hole open so the wound can drain. Then Dr. Harlow "dresses" the wound, pulling the loose skin back into position and taping it in place with adhesive strips. He puts a compress bandage directly over the wound and pulls Phineas's nightcap down tightly over it. Finally he winds a roller bandage around his forehead to hold all the bandages securely. Only then does he notice Phineas's hands and forearms, which are black with powder burns. Dr. Harlow dresses the burnt skin and has Phineas put to bed with his head elevated. He gives strict orders that his patient is to remain in that position.

Phineas should have been dead long before this. A thirteen-pound iron rod through the head should kill a person instantly. Surviving that, he should have died of shock soon after reaching Cavendish. He's lost a lot of blood, yet he remains awake and talkative. Even surviving the loss of blood, Phineas should have died of brain swelling. Any hard blow to the body causes injured tissue to swell. The brain is soft, and the skull is hard. A hard blow to the head can rattle the brain around inside like a BB in a tin can. The rattling bruises the brain, and bruised tissue swells. The brain swells, but the skull stays the same size; a swollen brain can jam itself so tightly it will cut off its own blood supply. This swelling can choke off oxygen to parts of the brain long enough to cause permanent damage. It can also cause death.

That's a "closed brain" injury (sometimes called a concussion). The possibility of a closed brain injury is why doctors fuss if you bang your head falling off a bicycle or crashing a car or getting hit hard in the head with anything. (To prevent closed brain injuries, you should wear a helmet when bicycling, driving a race car, fighting in the infantry, playing tackle football, parachuting, exploring a cave, working on a construction site, or doing just about anything where you could strike your head hard. In Phineas's case, however, a helmet would not have helped.)

Here Phineas has a stroke of luck. His is an "open brain" injury. The hole on top of his head gives his battered brain swelling room. The bad news is that his brain is open to infection. At first, though, he does remarkably well. The bleeding from his forehead slows and then stops within twenty-four hours. He remains cheerful and tells Dr. Harlow that he "does not care to see his friends, as he shall be at work in a few days." The morning after the accident, however, he is glad to see his mother and uncle when they arrive from New Hampshire. Two days after the accident, he takes a turn for the worse. He develops a fever and begins to have delirious spells. His wound is leaking a foul-smelling liquid, a sure sign of infection. His death seems just a matter of time now.

More than any other organ, the brain is sealed off from the outside world and from the rest of the body. There are many layers of tissue, bone, and skin to keep it protected from the outside, but there's also a "blood-brain barrier" that keeps out many substances circulating in the blood. Oxygen and nutrients can cross the blood-brain barrier, but many dangerous substances like bacteria cannot. With his skull fractured, Phineas's exposed brain is wide open, making him an ideal candidate for a fatal infection. No one in Cavendish in 1848, no scientist in America or Europe, has the slightest notion that bacteria cause infection.

Medical science in 1848 knows very little about bacteria, even though they were first seen through microscopes nearly two hundred years before. Today we are used to seeing the microscopic world, but when the microscope was invented in the middle of the seventeenth century, it caused a sensation. The microscope became a new kind of "high-tech" entertainment for cultured gentlemen, and in 1665 an Englishman named Robert Hooke came up with a microscopic "hit." He showed off a slide he'd made of an extremely thin slice of cork. Under the microscope lens, Hooke saw that the tissue inside a cork tree was made up of rows of tiny, boxlike structures. They reminded him of the bare rooms used by monks in a monastery. Hooke called them "cells." His cork cells, though, were empty because they were dead and dried out. It would take two centuries to figure out that it's the living stuff inside cells that makes them the fundamental unit of life.

While Hooke was showing off his "cells," a sharp-eyed Dutch merchant named Anton van Leeuwenhoek was making more powerful microscopes. Leeuwenhoek took a single drop of water from a rain barrel and turned his microscope on it. In that drop of water, Leeuwenhoek found a whole new planet of very, very small life forms. "Animalcules," he called them. Leeuwenhoek was the first to see single-celled micro-organisms, tiny plants and tiny animals, including bacteria. Yet Leeuwenhoek never had the faintest suspicion that some of his "animalcules" caused humans to sicken and to die.

That's more or less the state of knowledge in 1848. Few doctors have ever used a microscope, because it is not considered a medical instrument.

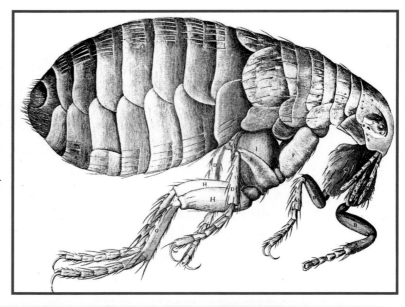

In 1665, the English scientist Robert Hooke published this detailed drawing of a flea as seen through the newly invented microscope. London society clamored to see more microscope images of things too fine for the human eye.

These microscopic animals might be marvels of nature, but no doctor suspects that they have anything to do with disease, let alone infections. Doctors in 1848 don't use the word *infection*, but they know its symptoms well. They call it "sepsis," and they know from bitter experience how quickly a "septic" wound can go from slight redness to gross swelling to a fatal condition called gangrene.

The doctors of 1848 don't realize that gangrene is the end result of bacterial infection. They don't realize that floating in the air on dust particles, lurking on fingertips, or growing on the shiny steel blades of their unwashed surgical scalpels are single-celled bacteria and other microscopic life forms. On the smallest surface, there are hundreds of millions of them. They represent thousands of different species; there are tiny plants, tiny fungi, tiny viruses, and tiny animals. Among the microanimals are two particularly dangerous families of bacteria—streptococci and staphylococci ("strep" and "staph," for short). What doctors don't know in 1848, strep and staph do: that the broken head of Phineas is an ideal location to land.

A wound is an open door. A cut or break in the skin lets staph and strep bacteria colonize the warm, wet, nutrient-rich cells inside. Once these bacteria get established in the body, they reproduce wildly. The body's immune system tries to kill the invading bacteria with an array of special immune cells, while the bacteria try to protect themselves against immune cells by cranking out toxic chemicals. That's an infection. The site of this biological battle between the immune system and bacteria swells up and turns red.

In 1848, science is still twenty years away from figuring out that infections are the work of living—that is, "biotic"—things. It will take nearly a century for science to develop the first "antibiotic," penicillin, to counter infections. In 1848, a young Frenchman named Louis Pasteur is still studying chemistry in Paris. Eventually, Pasteur will unravel the three great biological mysteries of his time—fermentation, decay, and infection. All three processes are the work of living microorganisms; Pasteur will call them "germs." Pasteur's "germ theory" will lead to a revolution in medicine. It will inspire an English surgeon named Joseph Lister to try performing surgery in sterile conditions that exclude or kill all microorganisms. Lister will scrub his hands almost raw before operating, he will boil surgical clothing and instruments, and he will set up a machine to spray carbolic acid in the operating room to kill germs in midair. Lister's first sterile operations in 1868 will cut the number of deaths from infection after surgery by 90 percent. For the first time in history, doctors will help more patients with surgery than they harm with postsurgical infections.

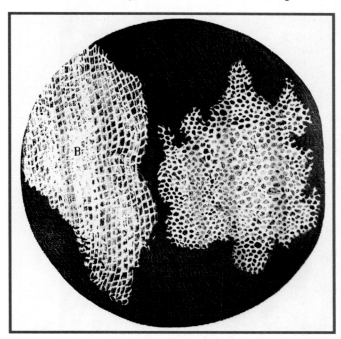

Hooke called the microscopic boxes that he saw in the bark of a cork tree "cells." Compared to his flea pictures, Hooke's cells attracted little notice in 1665. Two centuries later, his "cells" turned out to be the fundamental unit of all life.

None of this progress to come will do Phineas a bit of good back in 1848. Instead, Phineas is saved by good luck and good care. Dr. Harlow follows the best medical advice of his time—keep the wound clean but covered and watch for inflammation. A sign of infection is a fluid called "pus" (it's actually dead white blood cells, a sign that the body's immune system is attacking bacterial invaders) that collects in pockets to form abscesses. Fourteen days after the accident, Phineas develops a huge abscess under the skin just above his eyes. Phineas is feverish, losing his appetite, and sinking fast. Dr. Harlow lances (punctures) the abscess. He drains the pus and dresses Phineas's forehead again. The fever abates. His scalp begins to heal.

Phineas is saved by his youth, his iron constitution, and Dr. Harlow's good nursing. Dr. Harlow will always be modest about his role in saving Phineas. "I dressed him," Dr. Harlow will say. "God healed him."

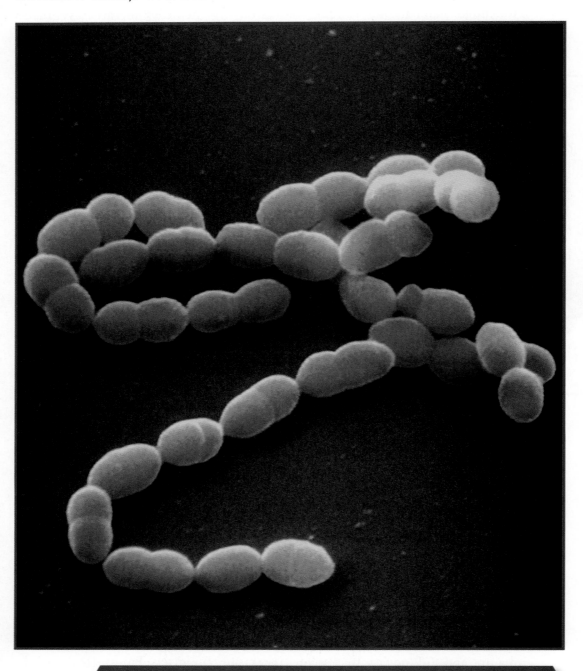

Under the microscope, streptococci bacteria have a distinctive beads-on-a-string appearance. "Strep" bacteria live on nearly everything people touch but are only dangerous if they can penetrate the body's defenses and overpower the immune system.

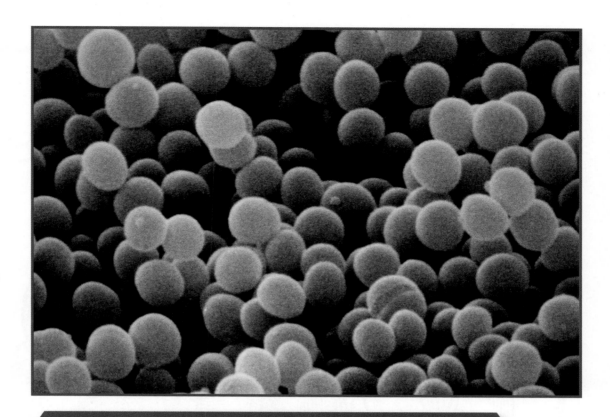

Staphylococci bacteria are the other half of the deadly duo of opportunistic bacteria. Infections by "staph" and "strep" were a leading cause of death before the discovery of antibiotic medicines. Somehow, Phineas's immune system beat off their attack.

The patient gains strength. Too much strength, in his doctor's opinion. Dr. Harlow is called out of town for a few days, and when he comes back he finds Phineas out of his sickbed. His head still heavily bandaged, Phineas is roaming about Cavendish in the rain with no coat and thin shoes. He is eating unwisely, refusing nursing advice, and ignoring doctor's orders. Phineas says he wants to go home to his mother's house in Lebanon, New Hampshire, twenty miles away. He intends to walk. According to the best medical theories of his day, Dr. Harlow diagnoses an imbalance of bodily "humors." This theory, which goes back to the ancient Greeks, declares that health is maintained by a balance of four liquids, or humors, in the body—blood, phlegm, yellow bile, and black bile. To bring them into balance, Dr. Harlow prescribes two powerful drugs—an "emetic" to make Phineas throw up and a "purgative," a powerful laxative, to evacuate his bowels. Phineas is knocked flat by the medicines and spends the next two weeks in bed, where Dr. Harlow keeps him on a "low," or bland, diet. His humors may or may not be in balance, but Phineas is resting quietly at last.

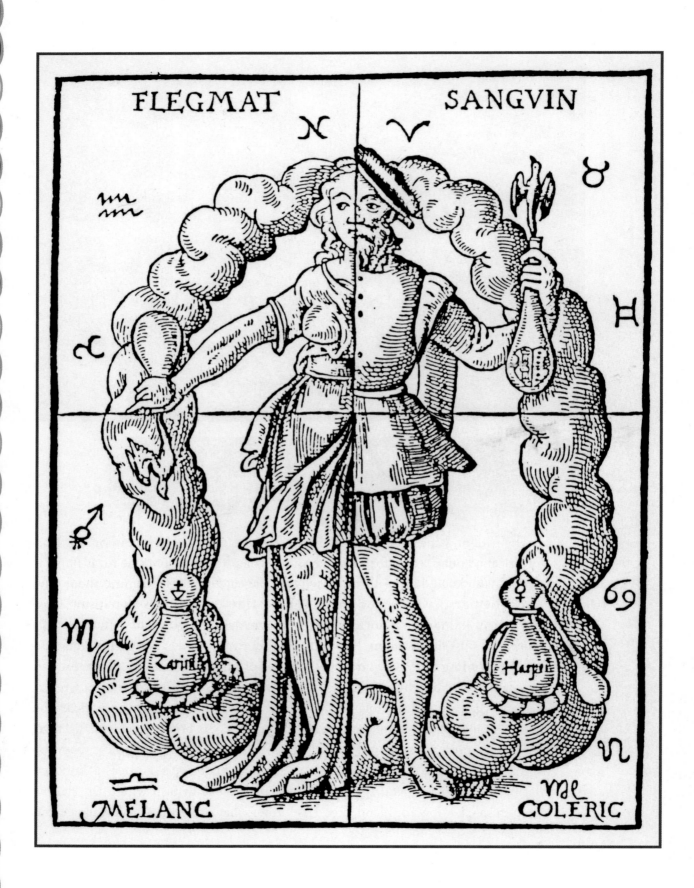

FLEGMAT

SANGVIN

MELANC

COLERIC

Phineas Gage

Ten weeks after the accident, Dr. Harlow declares Phineas fully recovered from his wounds. He puts Phineas in a closed carriage and sends him home to his mother in New Hampshire. Phineas is very weak, but he can walk short distances. He can count, feed and dress himself, and sing. He can speak clearly and make sense of what he hears. Yet there is something odd about the "recovered" Phineas. Just before he leaves Cavendish, Dr. Harlow gives Phineas a little test. The doctor offers Phineas $1,000 for the pocketful of pebbles that Phineas has collected walking along the Black River near town. Dr. Harlow knows that Phineas can add and subtract, yet Phineas angrily refuses the deal. Dr. Harlow tells himself that a man who was so badly hurt is going to need time to regain his full powers.

As soon as Phineas leaves for home, Dr. Harlow writes a short report for the *Boston Medical & Surgical Journal*. Most doctors ignore Dr. Harlow's article. The few who read it don't believe it. How could a man survive such an injury, let alone make a "complete recovery"? But one Boston doctor is intrigued. He writes to Harlow for information and urges the Vermont doctor to back up his case by collecting formal statements from eyewitnesses in Cavendish. The letter is from Henry J. Bigelow, professor of surgery at the Harvard Medical College.

In the spring, Phineas is back in Cavendish, carrying his tamping iron. He never goes anywhere without it these days. Phineas has come for a final examination by Dr. Harlow and to reclaim his old job on the railroad. His left eye looks intact, but the vision has gradually faded away. Phineas has a huge scar on his forehead and a small scar under his cheekbone, but otherwise he is physically healed. Yet Dr. Harlow has private doubts about Phineas's mental state. Phineas is just not his old self.

His old employers on the railroad quickly come to the same conclusion. The new Phineas is unreliable and, at times, downright nasty. He insults old workmates and friends. He spouts vulgar language in the presence of women. He changes his mind and his orders from minute to minute. The railroad contractors let him go. Dr. Harlow, who is keeping confidential notes on Phineas, sadly writes, "His contractors, who regarded him as the most efficient and capable foreman in their employ previous to his injury, considered the change in his mind so marked that they could not give him his place again."

Phineas Gage

When he was an old man, Dr. Henry J. Bigelow wore a long beard and sober clothes, befitting one of Boston's senior surgeons. But when he was a young man studying medicine in Paris, Bigelow was a snappy dresser.

Phineas's old friends also wash their hands of him. Dr. Harlow writes: "He is fitful, irreverent, indulging at times in the grossest profanity (which was not previously his custom), manifesting but little deference for his fellows, impatient of restraint or advice when it conflicts with his desires." Phineas comes up with all sorts of new plans, the doctor writes, but they are no sooner announced than he drops them. Phineas is like a small child who says he is running away from home after lunch and then comes up with a new idea over his sandwich. Dr. Harlow writes, "A child in his intellectual capacities and manifestations, he has the animal passions of a strong man." A doctor is bound by his oath not to reveal the details of a patient's condition without permission, so Dr. Harlow will keep his observations to himself for twenty years.

Meantime, Dr. Harlow has another letter from Dr. Bigelow at Harvard, who thanks him for collecting the eyewitness statements about the accident. Would Mr. Gage consider coming to Boston at Dr. Bigelow's expense so his case could be presented at the medical school and before the Boston Society of Medical Improvement? Dr. Harlow and Dr. Bigelow make arrangements.

What We Thought About How We Thought

In the winter of 1850, Phineas goes to Boston so the doctors there can see for themselves. What are doctors like in 1850? They look like gentlemen, or at least they do in the oil portraits that they have painted of themselves to boost their social status. If you lined up a gallery of these doctors' portraits, you'd see a long row of wise faces, satin waistcoats, gold watch chains, and side-whiskers. By 1850, there are photographs of doctors, showing wise faces, satin waistcoats, and whiskers. Photographs of doctors at work, though, are rare. Photographing anyone or anything moving is difficult because the light-sensitive plates are very slow, and a single exposure can take a full minute. Yet the year before Phineas's accident, a Boston photographer named Josiah Hawes sets up his camera in a surgical operating theater and takes a "daguerreotype" (a photograph on a metal plate) that he entitles, "Third Operation Using Ether Anesthesia at the Massachusetts General Hospital." The operating room is called the Ether Dome and still exists today.

The picture that Hawes makes is probably the very first of doctors being doctors instead of doctors posing for portraits. In Hawes's photograph, the surgeons stand impatiently beside the operating table, ready to start work. This is truly a historic moment. Before the introduction of ether a few months before, surgeons had to employ powerful assistants to hold down patients or restrain them with leather-covered chains. Because of the discovery of ether anesthesia, the doctors in the Ether Dome can take their time operating.

Notice two things about Hawes's picture. First, it's all men. There are no female hospital nurses, let alone female doctors. The second thing you should notice is what the doctors are wearing—nothing special. They are in street clothes—black frockcoats, shiny satin vests, and linen shirts. No one is wearing surgical scrubs. No one is wearing surgical gloves, masks, or booties. These doctors may not wash their hands until *after* the operation. These men know nothing about bacteria—but they think they know all about the brain.

This is what an audience of doctors looks like when Phineas arrives in Boston in January 1850, tamping iron in hand. He is Dr. Bigelow's guest but also his prize specimen. Phineas is examined, measured, and discussed. He agrees to sit for a plaster "life" mask. Dr. Bigelow puts straws up Phineas's nose so he can breathe while the doctor pours liquid plaster over his face. Then the plaster is lifted off to make a mold. From it, Dr. Bigelow casts a three-dimensional version of Phineas's face. His eyes are shut, but the enormous scar on his forehead is clear.

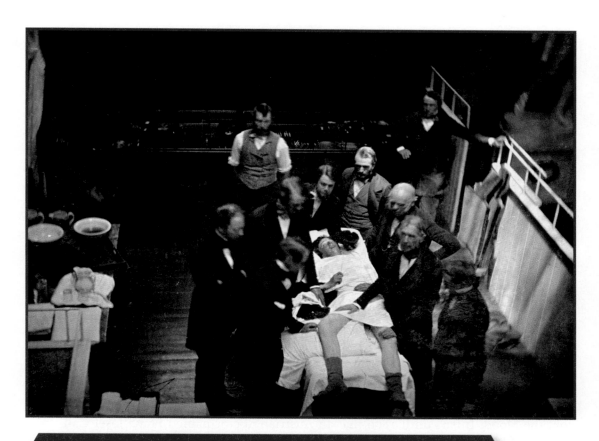

The patient is the one in the cotton gown and wool socks, lying unconscious on the table. Knocked out by inhaling ether fumes, the patient can feel no pain in this state of "twilight sleep." When word of the discovery of anesthesia reached England, a London newspaper rejoiced, announcing, "We Have Conquered Pain."

Phineas appears in person at Dr. Bigelow's lectures to convince the assembled doctors that his case is neither an exaggeration nor a fraud. Dr. Bigelow tackles that question head-on: "The leading feature of this case is its improbability," Dr. Bigelow admits. "A physician who holds in his hand a crowbar, three and a half feet long, and more than thirteen pounds in weight, will not readily believe that it has been driven with a crash through the brain of a man who is still able to walk off, talking with composure and equanimity of the hole in his head. Yet there is every reason for supposing it in this case literally true."

The evidence is standing before them, "crowbar" in hand. Even confronted with that, there are still doctors in the audience who don't believe that the tamping iron went through Phineas's brain. Perhaps, they say, it just hit him a glancing blow on the head. Dr. Bigelow reads out accounts from Dr. Williams and Dr. Harlow. He adds other eyewitness statements from Cavendish people including Mr. Adams, the hotel owner, and some of Phineas's workmen. Dr. Bigelow unveils his plaster life mask of Phineas. The casting clearly shows scars where the iron went in and came out. Yet there are doctors who think that Phineas is a humbug, a fake from the back woods of Vermont.

There are two other groups of doctors paying close attention to Dr. Bigelow's presentation. The two rival groups are eager to believe in Phineas's case. Their theories directly contradict each other, and yet both groups believe that Phineas's case supports their side. As it turns out, both groups are slightly right but mostly wrong. Yet their wrong theories—and Phineas himself—will steer our knowledge of the brain in the right direction.

Everybody knows that people use their brains to think. Right? And, of course, emotions, especially love, come from the heart. Wrong? Obviously, our ideas about how the body works have changed. Three hundred years ago, everybody "knew" that anger was controlled by the spleen. Twenty-three hundred years ago, the ancient Greeks "knew" that the heart was the center of emotion and thought. Aristotle, the greatest scientist of his time, "knew" that the primary function of the brain was to cool the blood. It isn't until 1800 that an Austrian doctor named Franz Josef Gall declares that the brain is the seat of the intelligence, the emotions, and the will. Still, it takes time for new ideas to sink in. Even today, we don't talk about a lover who's been dumped as feeling "broken-brained."

By Phineas's time, doctors know what a brain looks like, at least from the outside. They learn as students of gross (a term for "large-scale") anatomy by dissecting the cadavers of paupers, prisoners, and the unclaimed. By 1850, all doctors know the gross anatomy of the skeleton, internal organs, muscles, and, of course, the brain. They just don't know how the brain works.

You can have a look for yourself. Imagine you could click open the top of your head and lift your brain out. It weighs about three pounds. Some compare it to half of an enormous walnut, but if you can't visualize a three-pound walnut half, think of a bicycle helmet (bicycle helmets look the way they do so they can surround the brain). Think of your brain as a big cap perched on a stalk and protected by the neck flap. The big cap is your cerebral cortex. The stalk is your brain stem, which plugs into your spinal cord. The brain stem keeps many of your automatic functions going, like your breathing and heartbeat. The neck flap covers your cerebellum, which coordinates movement. Without your cerebellum, you couldn't walk upright, touch your finger to your nose, or turn this page. Without your brain stem, you couldn't breathe. Without your cerebral cortex, you wouldn't be human.

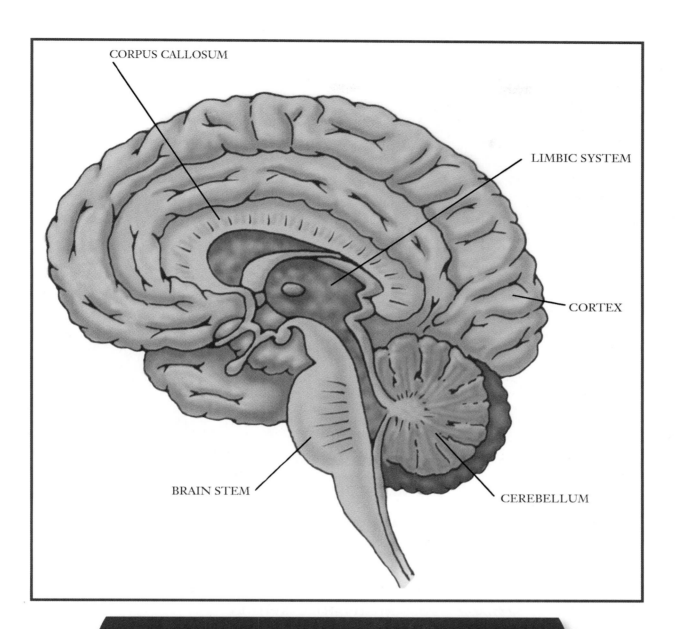

CORPUS CALLOSUM

LIMBIC SYSTEM

CORTEX

BRAIN STEM

CEREBELLUM

This is half a brain. On top and in front is the cortex. In the back and underneath are the cerebellum and the brain stem. On the bottom of the cortex is the limbic system, which coordinates memory, sensation, and emotion. In Phineas's case, the tamping iron passed through the frontal cortex, leaving the rest of his brain relatively unharmed.

What We Thought About How We Thought

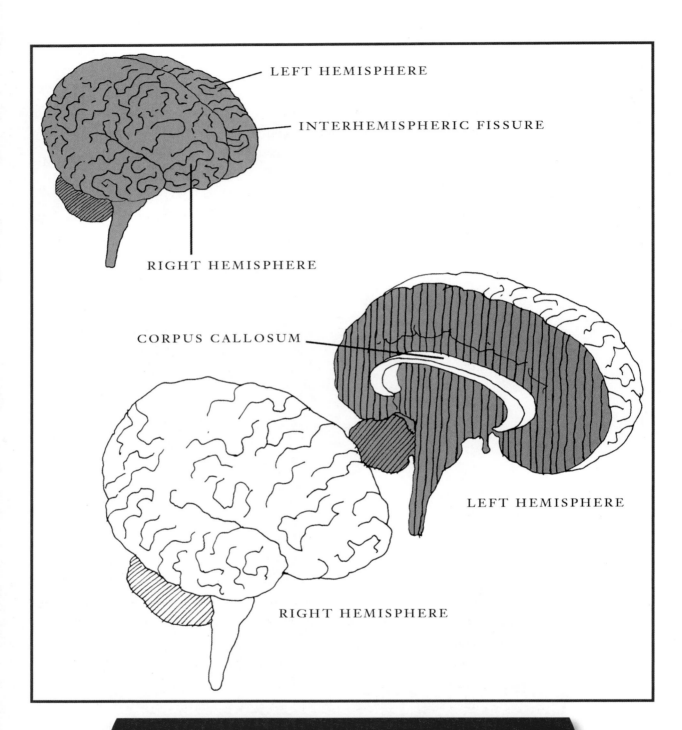

LEFT HEMISPHERE

INTERHEMISPHERIC FISSURE

RIGHT HEMISPHERE

CORPUS CALLOSUM

LEFT HEMISPHERE

RIGHT HEMISPHERE

Here you can see the division between the two hemispheres of the cortex. The crack between them is called the "interhemispheric fissure." The two hemispheres specialize in different mental skills, but brain functions are not as neatly divided as they appear. Phineas's tamping iron struck the left hemisphere first but also grazed the right hemisphere on the way out. He lost something from both hemispheres.

Phineas Gage

The cortex is where you think, remember, learn, imagine, read, speak, listen, and dream. In the cortex, you feel your emotions and you make sense of what your senses are telling you. The cortex is where you actually see what your eyes transmit, smell what your nose senses, taste what your tongue samples, touch what your nerves report, and hear what your ears pick up. None of this vital activity is visible in gross anatomy. By just holding a brain in your hands you (and the doctors of Phineas's day) can't see the thing that makes this organ work, the brain's fundamental unit, which is the brain cell, or neuron. You'll need a microscope and a lot of skill to see a single neuron, but all of these structures—the cortex, cerebellum, brain stem, and spinal cord—are made up of neurons specialized to relay and transmit tiny electrical impulses. By layering and connecting billions of neurons, you get a brain.

But by looking at your brain in your hand, you'll notice that the cortex splits in half right down the middle. The left hemisphere and the right hemisphere are separated on top by a deep crack—the interhemispheric fissure—but joined in the middle of the brain by a thick mat of nerves—the corpus callosum. The corpus is the switchboard for signals back and forth between the two halves. In recent times, scientists have learned that the two hemispheres specialize in certain skills. Sometimes you'll hear brain researchers talk about a "right brain" or a "left brain" skill. They really mean right or left hemisphere. But you can't see any skills by looking at the outside of a brain.

Indeed, if you're looking at your brain from the outside, you might wonder if you're holding the cortex backwards. The front of the cortex seems to be hanging in space until you realize that your face fits the space underneath. The part of the cortex above your face is the frontal lobe. The frontal lobe is the part that concerns us most regarding Phineas, but you should know the other lobes—the parietal lobe on top and the occipital lobe at the back of your head, right above your cerebellum. Wrapping around your temples on the side of your head are the temporal lobes. Each hemisphere has its own frontal, parietal, occipital, and temporal lobes. All together, the cortex is a soft mass of folded nerve tissue. It looks as if your cortex was folded up quickly and stuffed in any old way, but the truth is that every human brain is folded in exactly the same way. How the neurons inside those folds and ridges connect is what makes every human being singular.

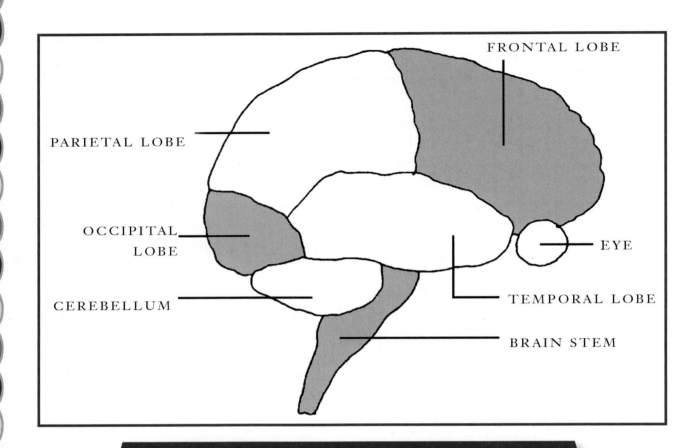

FRONTAL LOBE

PARIETAL LOBE

OCCIPITAL LOBE

CEREBELLUM

EYE

TEMPORAL LOBE

BRAIN STEM

The brain cortex is like a city; every part has an address. Instead of a city's east or west side, the cortex has a left and right hemisphere. The folds and ridges in the hemispheres are like cross streets, and medical students must memorize every one. The cortex also has four lobes—the frontal (in front), the parietal (on top), the occipital (at the back), and the temporal (on the side). A brain "address" can specify left or right hemisphere, the lobe, the nearest ridge or fold, and whether the location is on top or bottom, inside or out, and front or back. Phineas was injured most seriously on the inside of the left frontal lobe, but scientists are still arguing about the exact address.

After this tour of the outside of the brain, what you and the Boston doctors in 1850 still lack is a map of the nerve cells. In 1850, the Boston doctors know very little about any kind of cell, even though the cell revolution is getting under way in

Germany, thanks to Matthias Schleiden and Theodor Schwann. Working independently, they both revisit the work of Robert Hooke, the microscope observer who came up with the name *cell* in 1665. Hooke, they realize, was seeing empty cork cells because they were dead. Now, for the first time, Schleiden sees living cells in plants. Schwann sees them in animal tissue. Together, they realize that the cell is the fundamental unit of life. Everything alive, from slime molds to human beings, is composed of cells. It is the stuff inside the cell that controls every process of life, from digestion to reproduction.

As a living organism becomes more complex, its cells *differentiate*—that is, they specialize. A line of cells will differentiate and become muscle cells. Another will differentiate and become nerve cells. All complex animals have nerve cells, but no animal has as many nerve cells as humans do. Your brain and spinal cord have about 100 billion neurons.

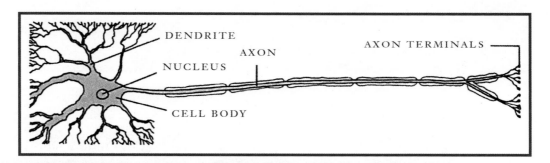

The nerve cell, or neuron, is a living, one-way wire with switches at both ends. Messages arrive chemically in the dendrites, where they are converted to electrical impulses, which travel down the axon, the long body of the cell. At the terminal on the far end, signals are converted back into chemical messengers, called neurotransmitters, for the short voyage across the synapse to the dendrites of the next neuron. Amazingly, neurons can work as fast as thought.

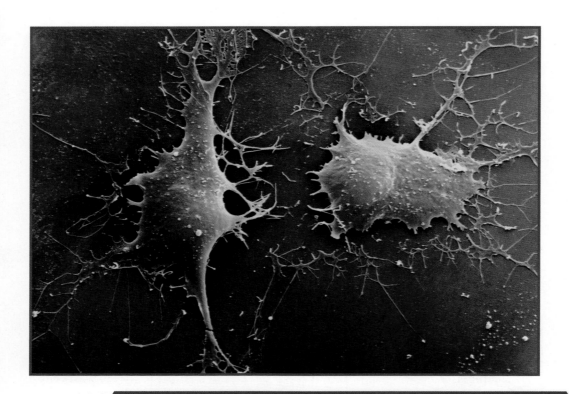

Here two human nerve cells show off their intricate network of axon terminals and dendrites. These connections are so fine that they cannot be seen through a conventional light microscope. A scanning electron microscope (SEM) was used here to capture the details.

A neuron is basically a wire with plugs at each end. Unlike most wires, most neurons have many, many plugs so they can both relay messages and switch them. A neuron is a long, skinny cell with a tangle of receivers at one end called dendrites, a long connector called an axon in between, and at the other end a smaller tangle of transmitters called axon terminals. Neurons never actually touch one another or splice together. There is always a tiny gap between the axon terminal of one neuron and the dendrite of the next. The gap is called a synapse. It is bridged by signaling chemicals call neurotransmitters. A message travels as an electrical impulse through the axon, down the body of the nerve cell, to the axon terminal. There the electrical impulse is converted into a chemical neurotransmitter to float across the synapse to the next neuron. Here's where the complications begin. In your brain, your neurons have lots of choices. Your brain has lots of synapses because the neurons are layered and clumped together so that the number of possible connections is huge. Each neuron can have anywhere from 1,000 to 6,000 synapses. That means the 100 billion neurons in your brain and spinal cord have a possible 100 *trillion* synaptic choices to make. Complexity is good. Making synaptic connections is how your brain actually thinks, learns, remembers, acts, and reacts.

The Boston doctors watching Phineas in 1850 haven't a clue about neurons, which won't be discovered for another twenty years. Still, these doctors know that the brain sits atop the spinal cord, a thick, bundled cable of thousands of threads. Doctors do not know that each thread is a bundle of microscopic neurons. They do know that cutting the spinal cord results in paralysis. The higher the break in the spinal cord, the more complete the paralysis. They know that if the cord is cut at the base of the brain stem, the patient dies.

That's why Phineas interests the doctors. His injury is not at the back of his head in the cerebellum or at the bottom of the brain near the brain stem. He was struck through the forehead, and the iron must have pierced the frontal lobe of the cortex. If Phineas survived with a large piece of his cortex destroyed, then what does the cortex do? Across America and Europe, doctors are fiercely divided over this very question. These are the two rival schools. One group thinks the brain is a "whole intelligence," that is, that your brain is one interconnected "mind." Let's call them the "Whole Brainers." They think of the cortex as a chamber holding a formless cloud or jelly driven by a mysterious "vital force." Through this force, every part of the brain is connected to every other part. The Whole Brainers believe that thoughts and commands can originate anywhere in the brain jelly/cloud and flash into action. If one part of the brain is injured, then the functions or thoughts that came from there will flow to another part.

Unfortunately, the Whole Brainers have no hard evidence for their theory. Instead they must look for unusual cases that might back them up. Phineas seems to be such a case. Dr. Bigelow of Harvard thinks so. He is a Whole Brainer.

His opponents believe in "localized function"; that is, they believe that the brain is divided into specific areas that control specific things. Let's call them the "Localizers." They are followers of the Austrian Dr. Gall, who started the brain revolution by declaring that the brain was the seat of intelligence, emotions, and will. Dr. Gall called his brain science "phrenology" (a made-up Greek word). By any name, the Localizers, or Phrenologists, believe that "organs" inside the brain control specific functions. They draw up a model Phrenological Head to show the "organs" in their correct positions. The "Organ of Veneration [respect]" and the "Organ of Benevolence [kindness]," for example, are supposed to be just above the left eyebrow. (Remember where Phineas was hit by the iron? Stay tuned.) Unfortunately, the Phrenologists have no way of knowing which part of the brain controls what. "Benevolence" cannot be seen on the outside of the brain.

Later in the nineteenth century, scientists will discover that a weak electrical current applied to the exposed brain of a laboratory animal will make certain muscles twitch involuntarily and certain senses sharpen or go dead. In the early twentieth century, scientists will invent more sophisticated and less dangerous ways to "see" brain activity. Eventually they will chart the brain's electrical signals by attaching electrodes to the scalp for an "electroencephalograph," or EEG. The EEG plots amazing patterns of electrical activity that match specific areas of the brain with specific functions. Toward the end of the twentieth century, scientists will invent brain scanners that can "image" the electrical and chemical activity inside a living brain.

A Phrenological Head is definitely an eye-catcher—bald as a billiard ball and each "organ" carefully outlined and labeled. By the middle of the nineteenth century, a popular parlor game is "reading" one's character by feeling the skull for bumps and dips and then matching them to a head chart such as this one.

Back in 1850, the Localizers/Phrenologists haven't seen a single thought or brainwave. Still, that doesn't stop them from identifying thirty-seven "organs" of the brain. How do they do it? Bumps. That's right. Bumps on the head. The Phrenologists reason that if you have a strong organ, it will be big and project from your skull as a bump. If you have a weak organ, it will be small and you'll have a dip or depression in your skull. Run your hand over your own skull and you will find all sorts of knobs, bumps, dips, and so on. The Phrenologists decide that if you have a bump over your Organ of Amativeness, you are a person with a strong talent for physical love. If you have a dip or a depression over your Organ of Philoprogenitiveness (also known as parental love), you're not going to be fond of children.

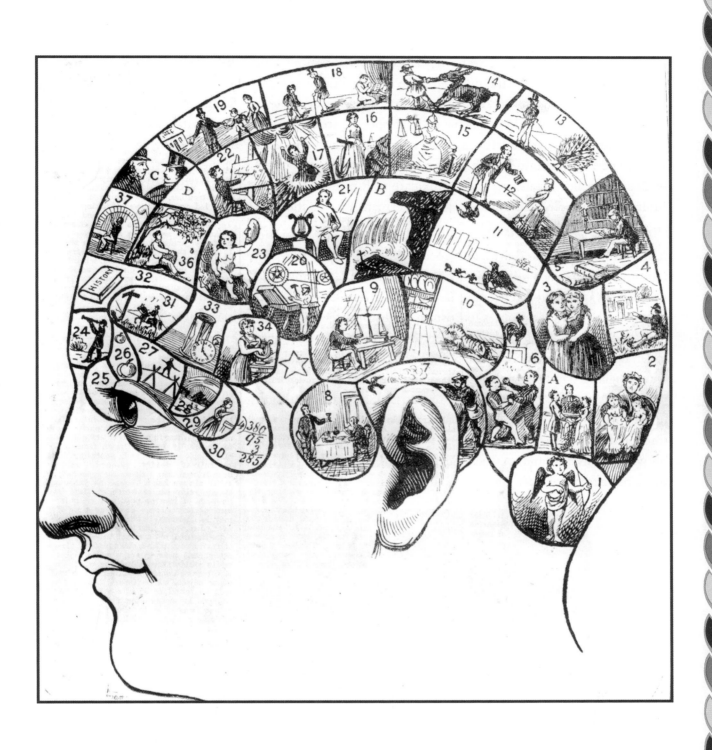

Among Boston doctors, phrenology is considered serious stuff when Phineas walks into the middle of the debate of the Whole Brainers versus the Localizers. Both sides seize him as proof of their belief. Dr. Bigelow and his fellow Whole Brainers say that Phineas would surely have died if specific areas of the brain were vital to specific functions. After all, the tamping iron carried away pieces of Phineas's brain. If every part of the brain was vital, then he should be dead. Yet here is Phineas alive in Boston, walking, talking, and taking care of himself. Therefore, say the Whole Brainers, the whole brain must be able to perform any function of one part.

On the other side, Dr. Harlow is a Localizer, or at least he is a friend of some leading Localizers/Phrenologists. The Localizers say Phineas proves their theory. The tamping iron has not killed him because the damage is limited to specific organs that are not critical to life. Yet the Localizers/Phrenologists don't have all the facts. In 1850, when Phineas comes to Boston, Dr. Harlow feels he must keep the details of his patient's personality problems confidential, but he does tell some of the truth to Dr. Nelson Sizer. Dr. Sizer is a big man in phrenology and lectures on it all over New England. Dr. Harlow leaks the information to Dr. Sizer that the "completely recovered" Phineas is not the old Phineas. Dr. Sizer tries to disguise the source of his report to the *American Phrenological Journal* in 1851, writing, "We have been informed by the best authority that after the man recovered, and while recovering, he was grossly profane, coarse, and vulgar, to such a degree that his society was intolerable to decent people."

An MRI scan allows us to look inside a living person's head and see a slice of everything from the throat to the spinal cord. Inside the brain, you can see the different lobes of the cortex; the corpus callosum, which joins the two hemispheres; the cerebellum at the back of the head; and the brain stem. Compare this to the phrenological chart on page 169.

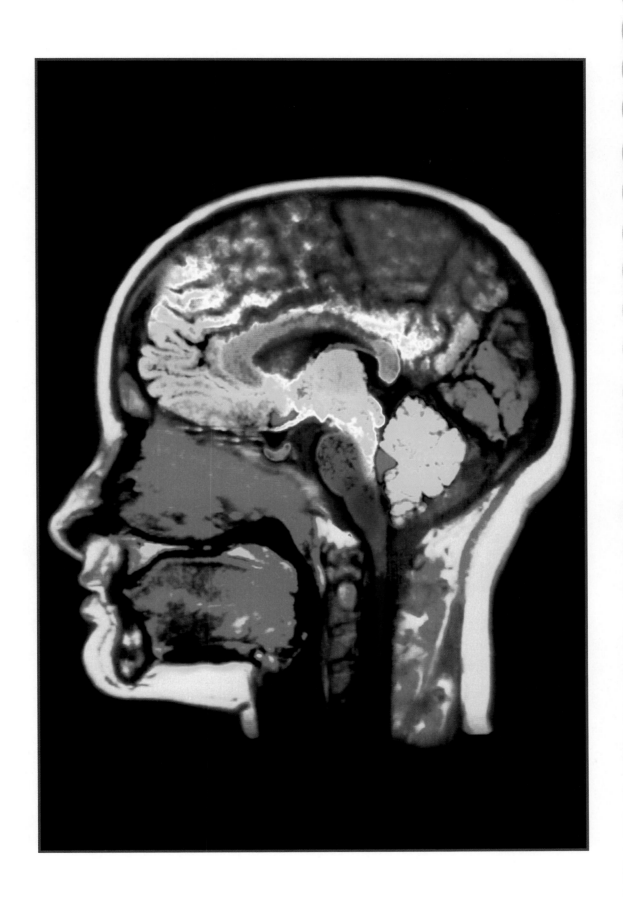

Dr. Sizer's report is wonderful news for the Localizers/Phrenologists. As Dr. Sizer explains, "If we remember correctly, the iron passed through the regions of the organs of BENEVOLENCE and VENERATION, which left these organs without influence in his character, hence his profanity, and want of respect and kindness."

In the long run, the Localizers will turn out to be somewhat right about localization but completely wrong about phrenological organs. The Whole Brainers will turn out to be right about the complex interconnections of the brain but wrong about the brain acting as a whole. The 100 billion neurons in your brain are not connected at random. They are organized into "local circuits" within the cortex; the local circuits form "subcortical nuclei," which together form "cortical regions," which form "systems," which form "systems of systems," which form you.

Specific areas of the brain do control specific functions and behaviors, but it's not always as "logical" as we would imagine. Skills that you think should be in the same brain patch are scattered about in different places in the cortex. Different areas of the cortex let you recognize letters in a book or faces in a crowd, or know whether you are standing upright. Yet many of these localized functions are also controlled by interactions with other parts of the brain. The human brain, it turns out, is both localized and interconnected. We know so much more about the brain today than the Phrenologists and the Whole Brainers did in 1850, yet we really understand only the rough outlines.

This ceramic bust by L. N. Fowler was to help serious phrenologists locate the thirty-seven "organs" of the brain while feeling around on the head for bumps and dips. Phrenology lost credibility as science found better ways to probe the brain. Compare this to the "coronal" MRI on page 193.

Back in 1850, Dr. Bigelow tells the Boston doctors, "Taking all the circumstances into consideration, it may be doubted whether the present is not the most remarkable history of injury to the brain which has been recorded." He also announces

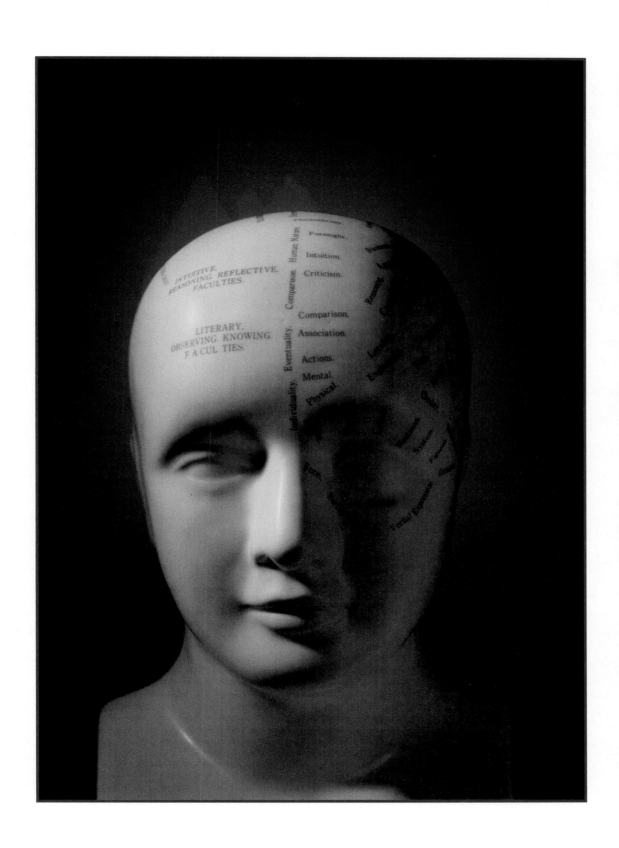

What We Thought About How We Thought

Around 1920, a group of Harvard Medical School students gather around the skull of Phineas Gage. The life-size plaster model of Phineas's head made by Dr. Bigelow stands on the left corner of the table. Time has made the skull fragile, but Phineas Gage's fame still draws visitors to Harvard's Countway Library to look without touching.

that Mr. Gage has graciously agreed to donate his famous tamping iron to the Harvard Medical College. Dr. Bigelow donates the plaster head of Phineas to go with it. The plaster head remains in Boston, but Phineas and his tamping iron soon slip out of town.

Following Phineas Gage

The story of Phineas Gage is famous, and when people repeat famous stories they have a tendency to improve them. The famous story about Phineas says that after hanging around the Boston medical school for weeks, he grows bored and restless. Phineas takes back his tamping iron and hits the road, traveling from city to city through New England and ending up at P. T. Barnum's American Museum on Broadway in New York City. Barnum's museum has nothing to do with our modern idea of a museum. It is a freak show.

In Barnum's time, people will pay to see "living giants," "bearded ladies," and calves born with two heads. People have always gawked at strange and unusual things. Barnum's special genius is "improving" the unusual. Hype and humbug make Barnum's museum a roaring success. He pulls in the crowds with half-fakes like the "Woolly Horse," a strange, long-haired horse that Barnum declares is a newly discovered species, being part deer, buffalo, elephant, camel, and sheep. At least the Woolly Horse is a real horse. Barnum's "mermaid" is a total fake, a counterfeit fossil pasted together from bones, withered skins, and who knows what else. Barnum shows his "mermaid" alongside real exotic animals like orangutans and grizzly bears. Barnum floods the exterior with the brightest lights in all of New York. Inside, the lighting is deliberately dim. The noise is deafening, with actors, jugglers, and glass blowers working the crowd.

In this wild scene, would anyone notice an ordinary-looking young man with a bad scar on his forehead holding an iron rod? It is said that Phineas exhibited himself and his tamping iron at Barnum's. The most colorful description of Phineas at Barnum's museum comes from Alton Blackington, a Boston radio and TV reporter who broadcasts his account a century after Phineas's death. Blackington says that Barnum's museum billed Phineas as "The Only Living Man with a Hole in His Head." According to Blackington, "The poster and one-sheets depicted a husky young man smiling broadly in spite of a huge iron bar which stuck out of his head. Actually, of course, the iron bar no longer protruded from Gage's head but he had it with him, and another skull, also perforated. During his sideshow performances, he would shove the long iron through the holes in his extra skull to demonstrate just how he was injured. All the details were to be found in a pamphlet he sold, and by paying ten cents extra, skeptics could part Gage's hair and see his brain, what there was left of it, pulsating beneath the new, thin covering."

Phineas Gage's mother said her son exhibited himself here at P. T. Barnum's American Museum on Broadway in New York City. Barnum was the gaudiest showman and greatest hoaxer of his age. Did Phineas Gage, The Man with a Hole in His Head, fit in with the other human oddities and strange wonders that Barnum promoted here with hype and hoopla?

Blackington spins a great yarn. Unfortunately, we don't know if the details are true. Phineas's mother did tell Dr. Harlow that after leaving Boston, Phineas and his tamping iron visited "most of the larger New England towns and New York, remaining a while in the latter place at Barnum's with his iron." But that's as far as the details go, and Blackington's sources can't be found. In our time, Professor Malcolm Macmillan, an Australian psychologist who is the world's leading expert on Phineas Gage, makes a massive effort to track down the story. Professor Macmillan turns to experts on Barnum, old newspaper files, contemporary diaries, and circus museums.

He can't find Phineas anywhere. As far as Professor Macmillan can determine, Dr. Harlow is the only reliable source. Dr. Harlow says that after Phineas leaves Boston in 1850 he gets information about his former patient only from Phineas's mother.

Her name is Hannah Trusell Swetland Gage. She says that Phineas returns from New York to the family's New Hampshire home early in 1851 to work for Mr. Jonathan Currier in his livery stable in the nearby town of Hanover. Whatever Phineas's problems with people, he gets on well with horses. He works in Currier's stable for a year and a half. His health is good, his mother remembers. He seems happiest with children and animals. Then, in 1852, he meets a stranger in Hanover who has big plans to set up a stagecoach line in South America between Valparaiso and Santiago, Chile. He could use a man who is experienced with horses. In August 1852, Phineas leaves New England forever, bound for Chile and a new life as a stagecoach driver.

Here the evidence fades out for a time. His mother recalls only that Phineas talked about driving six-horse teams for this coach line on the bottom of the world. She doesn't recall the stranger's name. But there is a small clue in the August 1852 order books of the Abbott-Downing Company of Concord, New Hampshire. In 1852, Abbott-Downing makes the finest and toughest stagecoach in the world. This Concord coach is the famous Wild West stage, hauling mail and passengers over the plains and across deserts. In 1852, the Abbott-Downing Company books show that a Mr. James McGill ordered a Concord stage for a new coach line that he was organizing in Valparaiso, Chile. Was James McGill the stranger who hired Phineas? Professor Macmillan is still looking for evidence in New Hampshire or Chile, but he says it's possible.

A Concord stagecoach is a monster on huge wooden wheels. With six horses, nine passengers, an armed guard, mail, and freight, a fully loaded Concord stage is over six tons in motion. The driver controls it all with reins, a whip, and a feeble wooden foot brake. It's not an easy job. The driver's fists are filled with reins, three pair in the left hand for the "near" side horses, three in the right for the "off" side. The whip is largely for making showy, whip-cracking arrivals in town. Mostly he drives with his hands and voice, using the matched pairs of horses to wheel, to slow down, or to pull clear.

Until Professor Macmillan turns up solid proof, we can't say for sure if Phineas drives a Concord stagecoach in Chile, but the driver's job would be much the same on any six-horse coach—hard, tiring, and sometimes exciting. According to his mother, Phineas drives for nearly seven years on a regular schedule over the primitive roads between Valparaiso and Santiago. There is so much we would like to know but probably never will about Phineas's time in Chile. Does he—can he—learn

Although it is being pulled by four horses instead of the usual six, this is a New Hampshire-built Concord stagecoach, somewhere in Chile at about the time that Phineas Gage arrived there. We have no way of knowing if it is Phineas at the reins.

Spanish? Is he a loner? Does he stay with the same stage line or jump from job to job? Does he tell anyone in Chile his tragic story?

If we can't know any of this, we can catch a glimpse of Phineas in the driver's seat, his fists full of reins, his face full of dust, his hat pulled down over his eyes against the Chilean sun. Phineas is intent on his team, on the slope of the road, and on the big, rocking coach. His decisions are quick and instinctive, based on long habit. He knows his horses. He knows his reins.

We know one other thing about Phineas in Chile. He has his tamping iron with him. Stowed under the seat or ready to hand, the tamping iron goes everywhere Phineas goes.

In 1859, Phineas washes up on his family's doorstep in San Francisco. His mother has moved to California from New Hampshire to be with her youngest daughter, Phebe, and her new husband, David Shattuck. In July, a very sick Phineas gets off a boat in San Francisco and somehow finds his way to the Shattuck house. Phineas is in "feeble condition," his mother says, much changed since she last saw him in New Hampshire. Phineas tells his mother that he is only suffering from the voyage. He had been terribly seasick on his first voyage from Boston to Chile in 1852, he tells her. He will get over this. It takes months, but he seems to fully recover.

In San Francisco, Phineas is not a good invalid. He hates resting. He has worked hard all his life, on the family farm, on the railroad, in the livery stable, and on the

Chilean stagecoaches. As Phineas gradually feels better, he wants to go right out and get back to work. Finally Phineas takes a job plowing for a farmer near the little town of Santa Clara. Phineas tells his mother that he has no trouble with the farm work, but he soon quarrels with the farmer. He moves to another farm, then another. Phineas is "always finding something which did not suit him in every place he tried," says his mother. That February, he is back in San Francisco for a visit. At the dinner table, he suddenly falls into "a fit."

A fit is an epileptic seizure. Epilepsy is not a disease but a complex of symptoms. Basically, a seizure is an electrical storm in your brain's nerve cells. It can begin in one area of the brain and spread to other regions, sometimes sending your muscles into involuntary convulsions. Seizures are relatively common; about one person in 200 will experience a seizure, mild or severe, at some time in life. But an epileptic seizure is only a symptom; the cause can be anything from a tumor, to an inherited genetic disposition to seizures, to a blow to the head. In our time, we control most epileptic symptoms with powerful drugs called "anticonvulsants," because uncontrolled seizures can cause their own brain damage.

By the time a seasick Phineas Gage staggered ashore here in 1859, San Francisco was still a frontier town on the farthest edge of the continent.

Phineas Gage

In 1860, severe epileptic seizures are not controllable. All the doctors in San Francisco can offer Phineas are theories, useless drugs, and nursing instructions. After that first seizure at his sister's dinner table, he recovers almost immediately with no memory of the fit or any ill effect. Within hours, he has two more seizures. In the morning, he wakes up feeling like his old self and insists that he has to get back to work. Back in Santa Clara, he switches farm jobs again. In May, he comes into San Francisco to visit his mother. He seems fine. Two days later, at five o'clock in the morning, Phineas has a severe seizure. Then he has another and another. The intervals between seizures grow shorter and shorter.

The family physician comes and "bleeds" him. By 1860, the practice of bleeding a patient is the last gasp of a treatment that goes back to the "bodily humors" theory of the ancient Greeks. The doctor who treats Phineas decides he has too much blood and draws off the "extra." It's outmoded treatment, even for 1860. Back in Vermont in 1848, Dr. Harlow bled Phineas at the height of his fever. Without understanding why, Dr. Harlow may have helped Phineas at the moment of crisis. Drawing blood reduces blood pressure slightly, which may have taken some of the pressure off his swollen brain. But bleeding does nothing for epileptic seizures.

Phineas's seizures are probably caused by slow changes in brain tissue damaged in the original accident. Why the damage worsens as Phineas grows older is unknown. Possibly Phineas strikes his head again. Perhaps the constant jarring in the driver's seat of a lumbering stagecoach causes a concussion on the site of the old damage. Perhaps Phineas has a low-grade bacterial infection or perhaps a brain tumor. No one can say why, but now Phineas's seizures grow more violent and more frequent. One after another, the seizures leave him weaker and weaker.

They finally kill him on May 21, 1860, at his sister's house in San Francisco. The immediate cause of death is probably hypothermia—his body can't control its internal temperature. In our time, we read about hypothermia killing mountain climbers, or sailors who fall into cold water. An epileptic seizure creates the same effect as shivering in icy water. In cold water, you shiver—your muscles spasm—to heat up your body. While shivering violently in cold water, you don't realize you are also sweating as your muscles throw off heat. Eventually the muscles expel heat faster than it can be replaced. Your blood temperature starts to fall. Your internal organs, especially the brain and heart, need a constant core temperature to function. As the brain detects a fall in blood temperature, it automatically protects itself by shutting down the blood supply to the hands and feet. You lose feeling. If you keep losing heat, the brain shuts down blood circulation over a larger and larger area of your skin. Phineas's muscle seizures are causing the same effect. His brain shuts down circulation to his feet and hands, then his skin, and then organ by organ until his brain must choose between blood for itself and blood for the heart. His heart stops. This is how Phineas dies, twenty days short of his thirty-seventh birthday.

He is buried at Laurel Hill Cemetery in San Francisco. Phineas is a stranger in the city, and few outside his family circle know anything about his curious past. No California newspaper notes his death or burial. Family news travels slowly across the continent. Back east, the country is drifting toward Civil War, and when it breaks out the following April, doctors soon have more pressing concerns than Phineas Gage.

Half the world away from San Francisco in 1862, French surgeon Paul Broca in Paris announces a discovery that finally turns brain theory into brain science. Dr. Broca shows how damage to one very small spot in the brain causes one very specific kind of damage. Broca is still unable to study a living brain, but he has been performing autopsies on the brains of stroke victims. A stroke is an interruption of the blood supply to the brain that causes localized damage and often leaves stroke patients without the ability to speak. Broca notices that in the brains of stroke patients who'd lost the power to speak there is visible damage in a small area on the outside of the left frontal lobe.

The spot becomes famous as "Broca's area." To find it, put your hand on the top of your left ear, directly above your ear hole. Move your fingers about two inches forward. Underneath the skull is your "Broca's area." If it's damaged, you will lose the ability to speak. In medical language, you will have "aphasia." Soon after Broca's announcement, a German named Carl Wernicke identifies a second area on the left temporal lobe that separately controls the ability to understand speech. The loss of the ability to understand what is said to you is called "receptive aphasia." Who could have imagined that these two skills would be controlled from two different places in the brain? Broca's and Wernicke's areas are the first anatomical proof of localization. Other brain researchers soon learn to use low-voltage electricity to stimulate specific points on the brain. Bit by bit, the map of the brain grows more detailed and more localized.

The new scientific map of the brain has no relation to our old friend the Phrenological Head. Phrenology falls into disgrace, even though the Phrenologists were right about localization. The Whole Brainers are also shaken. If speech is localized on these two spots, how could someone with massive frontal lobe injuries— Phineas Gage, for example—speak? And yet Dr. Harlow had said that Phineas had fully recovered. Of course, few doctors in Boston remember much about the Gage case, and even Dr. Harlow has lost track of Phineas.

By the time Dr. Harlow finds Phineas again, he is too late. After Phineas leaves for South America in 1852, Dr. Harlow's contact with the Gage family is broken.

The unquiet grave of Phineas Gage was disturbed once in 1867 by Dr. Harlow and then again in 1940 by the rapidly growing city. San Francisco needed the land under the old pioneer cemetery where he was buried. The remains of Phineas, his mother, his brother-in-law, and 35,000 other San Francisco pioneers were dug up by the city and moved to a mass grave in a suburban cemetery. Their headstones and tombs were trucked away for landfill. In 1944, a strong coastal storm uncovered the missing tombstones under a highway, and these boys scrambled up to see. If Phineas Gage had a tombstone, it was somewhere in this stone pile.

Quietly, he has wondered what became of his most celebrated patient. Then in 1866, the year after the Civil War ends, Dr. Harlow, now running a small practice in Woburn, Massachusetts, finds an address for Hannah Gage in San Francisco. He writes to her, and his letter makes the long trek across America. Mrs. Gage is delighted to hear from the doctor who'd done so much for her son. Unfortunately, she has the sad duty to report his death six years before.

It is too late for an autopsy, and California is too far for a research visit. But Dr. Harlow doesn't give up. They exchange cordial letters. Mrs. Gage describes Phineas's last illness. She fills in the details of his life after he left the medical spotlight in Boston. She recalls how Phineas was extremely fond of his little nephews and nieces. Dr. Harlow notes her description of how Phineas would entertain them "with the most fabulous recitals of his wonderful feats and hairbreadth escapes, without any foundation except in his fancy." Dr. Harlow concludes that Phineas had "a great fondness for children, horses, and dogs—only exceeded by his attachment for his tamping iron, which was his constant companion during the remainder of his life."

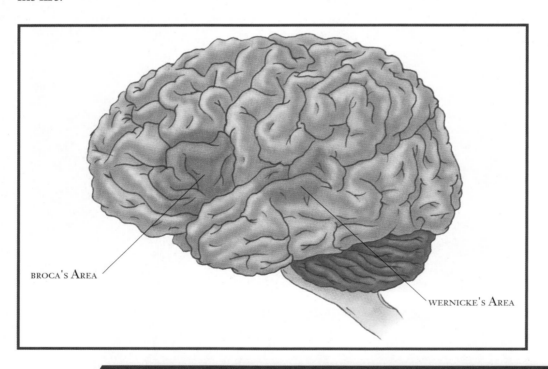

BROCA'S AREA

WERNICKE'S AREA

In 1862, Paul Broca found an area on the lower left frontal lobe that controlled the ability to speak. The discovery of Broca's area finished off the theories of the Phrenologists and the Whole Brainers. Soon after, Carl Wernicke found another area on the left temporal lobe that controlled the ability to understand speech.

Finally, Dr. Harlow makes an unusual request. Explaining the importance of her son's case to science, Dr. Harlow recalls how many scoffed at Phineas when Dr. Bigelow first presented his case in Boston. Now there is a way to settle the question, Dr. Harlow explains. Would Mrs. Gage allow her son's body to be exhumed—dug up—from his grave? Would she allow the skull to be removed and shipped to Massachusetts?

What a request. Surely Dr. Harlow must be held in the highest regard by Hannah Gage. Why else would she consent? With her son-in-law and the mayor of San Francisco, who happens to be a physician, standing by as witnesses, Phineas's coffin is

In his later years, Dr. John Martyn Harlow became an important man in Woburn, a state senator, an advisor to the governor, and a bank president. When he died in 1907, he left his large estate to various charities, including Middlesex County Medical Society. In 1998, the society had enough of Dr. Harlow's money left to help pay for the bronze monument to Phineas Gage on the town green in Cavendish, Vermont.

uncovered and carried to a shed. There, Dr. J. D. B. Stillman, a local surgeon, removes the skull. The huge fracture on the forehead is unmistakable. Dr. Stillman removes something else from the coffin—the tamping iron that Phineas carried everywhere, even to his grave. That December, David Shattuck takes the skull and tamping iron with him when he travels east on business. Early in the new year, he hands them over to an extremely grateful and very excited Dr. Harlow in Massachusetts.

At last Dr. Harlow is at liberty to tell the full story of Phineas Gage's "recovery" twenty years before. He appears before the Massachusetts Medical Society in 1868 and spills the beans. "This case has been cited as one of complete recovery . . . without any impairment to the intellect," he says, but in truth, Phineas's personality changed drastically after the accident. "Previous to his injury, though untrained in the schools, he possessed a well-balanced mind, and was looked upon by those who knew him as a shrewd, smart business man, very energetic and persistent in executing all his plans of operation. In this regard, his mind was radically changed, so decidedly that his friends and acquaintances said he was 'no longer Gage.'"

Phineas went from being "the most efficient and capable foreman" on the railroad to a man who couldn't be trusted because he couldn't get along with anyone. The new Phineas was pigheaded and stubborn one moment and wishy-washy and vague the next. "I think you have been shown that the subsequent history and progress of the case only warrant us in saying that physically, the recovery was quite complete," says Dr. Harlow. "Mentally the recovery certainly was only partial." The new Phineas could walk, drive a team of horses, and sail away to Chile, but he had lost a vital skill—he no longer knew how to be social.

Being social is a hard skill to measure. Social behavior goes beyond the ability to activate the correct muscles or decode the right spoken sounds. It's different from having manners. Manners are learned, and they differ greatly from culture to culture. Your parents teach you the "right" way to eat or to greet strangers, but other parents in other countries teach their children other "right" ways. Forks or chopsticks or fingers, there's no "right" way to put food in your mouth, yet all humans swallow the same way. Swallowing is automatic behavior. Using a fork is learned behavior. Eating politely in the company of others is social behavior.

It's hard to believe that this tamping iron shot through the skull without killing Phineas Gage. Dr. Harlow had their picture taken together in 1868 to document his case.

Phineas Gage

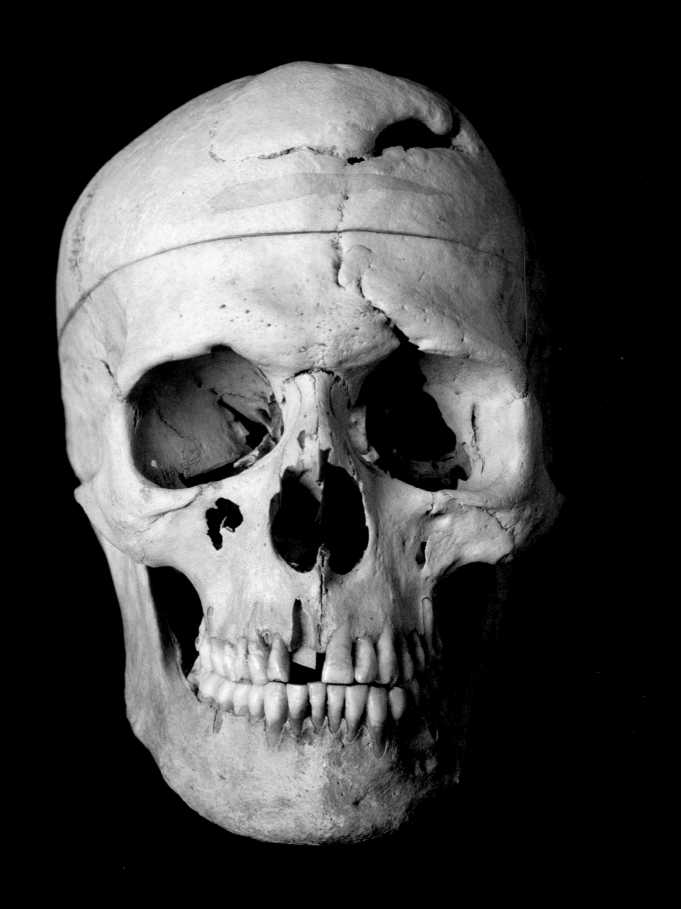

In death, Phineas's skull revealed the unmistakable signs of his terrible accident. Today, Phineas's skull, tamping iron, and life mask are exhibited at Harvard Medical School.

In your brain, Broca's area may let you speak and Wernicke's area may let you understand, but listening is also a complicated social behavior. Whether you realize it or not, you've been taught how to listen—how to make or break eye contact, how to murmur agreement or quiet objection, how to smile at the right moment or not to smile at all if the subject is grave. You also know how to show (or hide) your emotional reactions. You can laugh or yawn, roll your eyes upward in boredom, or open your eyes wide in delight. All of these behaviors can mean something entirely different in another culture, but all cultures have listening behavior.

To act human, you mix emotions, actions, routines, customs, manners, words, and expressions in a predictable way. That's what Phineas seems to have lost. Bossing a railroad construction gang requires more than a loud voice. A gang has to be able to "read" the social behavior of the foreman. They have to know if he's angry or just joking, if his orders are reasonable, or if his judgment can be trusted. He has to be able to "read" the social behavior of his men, to know who are the reliable ones and who are the troublemakers. By all reports, the old Phineas was an excellent foreman. The new Phineas was not. All these changes were brought on by a hole through a specific part of his brain.

In Boston twenty years before, the central exhibit had been Phineas himself, alive and seemingly well. Now Dr. Harlow reveals the clincher—his skull. He has "prepared" it for inspection, carefully sawing through the bone at just above eyebrow level so the top of the cranium can be lifted off. Now his audience can see the hole in the top of his mouth through which the rod passed. The top of Phineas's skull is an amazing sight. The doctors can see where Dr. Harlow pushed two large fragments back into place and how the edges started to regrow, unmistakable proof that Phineas survived the trauma and that his body started to heal the damage. Yet there is a visible hole in the top, a small triangular opening the size of a quarter, where the iron either smashed or carried away the bone completely. The skin closed over it, but for eleven years, Phineas had a real hole in his head.

At last, the true story of Phineas Gage is out in the open. The scientific debate about the brain, though, has moved on. The theories of the Localizers and Whole Brainers are being replaced by a new experimental brain science. In time, the pinpointing of control areas will become more and more detailed. Knowledge of cells in general and neurons in particular will transform understanding of the brain. Yet the truth about Phineas poses a question that no one seems eager to answer. If there are exact locations in the brain that allow for the ability to hear or to breathe, is there a place that generates human social behavior? If that place is damaged, do you stop acting human?

Phineas Gage

Putting Phineas Together Again

In our time, Phineas Gage is a textbook case. Students of neurology or psychology study his case because it illustrates how the lobes of the frontal cortex—the two halves of your brain that meet in your forehead—are the seat of "executive functions." Those are your abilities to predict, to decide, and to interact socially.

Unfortunately, Phineas is not the only person to have suffered damage to the frontal cortex. Antonio and Hanna Damasio, a husband-and-wife team of doctors, regularly see people who remind them of Phineas Gage. The Damasios are renowned brain researchers at the University of Iowa Hospitals & Clinics in Iowa City and treat patients with the same kind of frontal lobe damage that afflicted Phineas. Like Phineas, these patients with frontal lobe damage have trouble making decisions. Like Phineas with his $1,000 pebbles, they perform well on logic and math tests but make strange choices in trading situations. Their emotional responses are unpredictable. They seem out of step emotionally with the rest of the world.

The patients who come to the Damasios' clinic are not victims of blasting accidents. Their brain injuries usually follow surgery to remove a tumor from deep inside the frontal cortex. This kind of brain surgery is strictly a last resort to save a patient's life, because even if the operation goes well, the risk of side effects is high. Any damage to the frontal cortex can change behavior and personality forever, as the case of Phineas Gage demonstrates. Sometimes, cancer surgeons have no other choice. These cases are not common, but the Damasios have seen a dozen patients with many of the same symptoms as Phineas. All have frontal cortex damage. All have trouble making decisions on personal or social matters. All react with little empathy and seem to find emotion a foreign language.

To study these modern-day Phineases, the Damasios have far more sophisticated equipment than Dr. Harlow did. They have the full arsenal of CTs and MRIs—noninvasive brain scanners that can electronically "slice up" a brain and lay it out, level by level, like the floor plan of a house. But the Damasios also do simpler tests. Emotional response is difficult to measure, but there is one usually reliable sign of how you are feeling—sweaty palms. When your emotions are "aroused," your skin (all over and not just your palms) gets slightly warmer and slightly sweatier. Your sweat contains salts, which increase electrical conductivity. A person having a strong emotional reaction is going to "spike" a conductivity meter. It's the same principle used in the police "lie detector" test, only the Damasios are interested in a different sort of truth.

Hooked to a skin response machine, the modern-day Phineases are shown a series of emotionally charged pictures—a tranquil landscape, a beautiful woman, a severed foot. Their skin reactions are usually the same—nearly flat. The emotional colors of their world seem to have drained away. Another Damasio experiment involves a computer "gambling" game. There are four decks: A, B, C, and D. The decks are rigged. Normal subjects who play the game soon figure out that the C and D decks are better risks than A and B. The modern-day Phineases keep playing A and B, though they can explain to the experimenters mathematically exactly why C and D are better risks. They realize the game is rigged to favor a "slow but steady" strategy against a "risk-all" strategy, but they still play "risk-all." Call them Phineas's rules.

So what part of the brain controls this behavior? Dr. Harlow thought he had found the precise location of Phineas's troubles once he had the skull. By then, Phineas's actual brain was long gone, but Dr. Harlow knew enough gross anatomy to calculate that the iron had passed through the very front of the left frontal cortex. His answer was good enough for 1868. It isn't good enough today.

Studying the brain scans of these Phineas-like patients, the Damasios wonder what a brain scan of Phineas Gage himself would have shown. In 1994, Hanna Damasio has an idea of how to construct one retroactively. First she asks Dr. Albert Galaburda at the Harvard Medical School to have another look at Phineas's skull in the Harvard medical museum. Under the careful eye of the curators, Dr. Galaburda x-rays, photographs, and remeasures the skull. The results are digitized so the specifics of Phineas's skull can be overlaid onto a three-dimensional computer image of a generic human skull. Back in her lab in Iowa, Hanna Damasio carefully plots the entrance and exit wounds. A line is drawn between their center point to lay out a hypothetical path for the tamping iron. The generic electronic skull is then adjusted to Phineas's specifications. Now Dr. Damasio has Phineas's skull on a computer screen. She can tilt and rotate it in any direction exactly as if she were holding it in her hand.

Phineas Gage

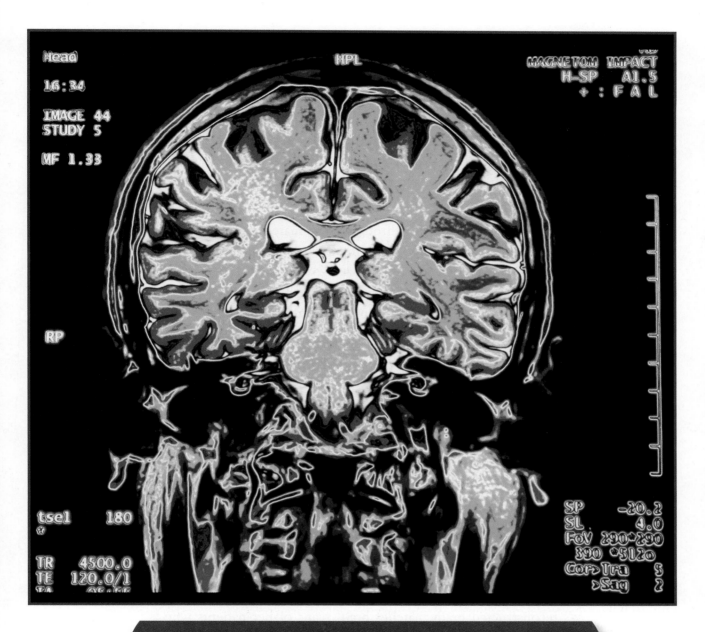

This is a "coronal" MRI. Instead of a side view, this is a slice of the brain taken head-on. Here we're somewhere in the middle of the head with the cortex above, the corpus callosum in the middle, and the brain stem descending to the spinal column.

Then she adds the tamping iron electronically. The real one tapers, but the electronic one is represented as a cylinder as big around as the fat end of the tamping iron. Now Dr. Damasio turns to a computer program called Brainvox that is used to reassemble brain scan "slices" into a three-dimensional model. Brainvox fits this electronically scanned brain inside Phineas's electronic skull.

Putting Phineas Together Again

The brain is a very small place, and a very small change in the path of the iron would have had very different results. Brainvox calculates sixteen possible paths for the iron to follow through Phineas's head. The anatomical evidence from Phineas rules out nine of these. Dr. Damasio knows that the iron missed his jawbone, lightly clipped the interior arch of his brow, and knocked out one molar but didn't destroy the socket. Any path that falls outside those landmarks is out of bounds. Of the remaining seven routes, two would have cut important blood vessels and would have killed Phineas instantly. Brainvox lays out the last five routes. The Damasio team whittles it down to one.

Brainvox plots it as a red cylinder passing through the animated computer skull. The top of the skull is open to show the rod emerging from the frontal cortex. It is a riveting image. The scientific journal *Science* puts Brainvox's images of the pierced skull on its cover and it causes a sensation. Whether you're a brain surgeon or a sixth-grader, the first time you see the Brainvox image of Phineas's head with that red bar through it, you wince.

If you study the animated skull from different angles, you can see Phineas's incredible luck. The iron passes through his head at a very steep angle. That's both his salvation and his ruin. It misses a number of key areas on the side and top of the brain. On the left temple, it misses Broca's area for speech. On top, it misses two key sections of the cortex, the motor and somatosensory strips. These areas integrate your sensory input and muscle actions so you keep oriented in space and in motion. Thus Phineas is left with the ability to keep his balance, to focus his attention, and to remember both old and new events.

The tamping iron, however, plows on through his frontal lobes, passing through the middle, where the two hemispheres face each other. The iron damages the left hemisphere more than the right, the front of the frontal cortex more than the back, the underside more than the top. Dr. Damasio recognizes the pattern. Phineas's reconstructed brain matches brain scans of her patients who had cortex tumor surgery.

The skull of Phineas Gage appeared on the cover of the journal *Science*. Generated by computer, the red bar plots the exact path of the tamping iron through his frontal cortex.

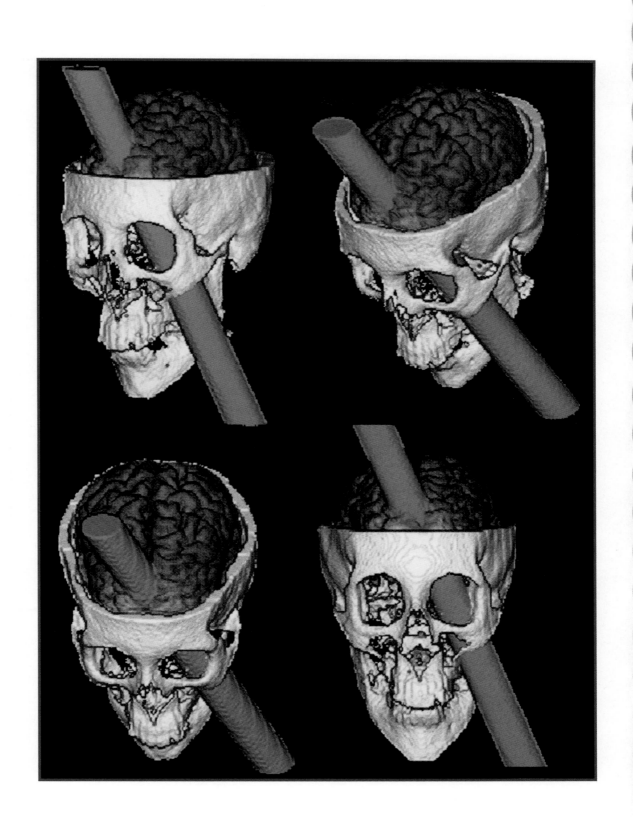

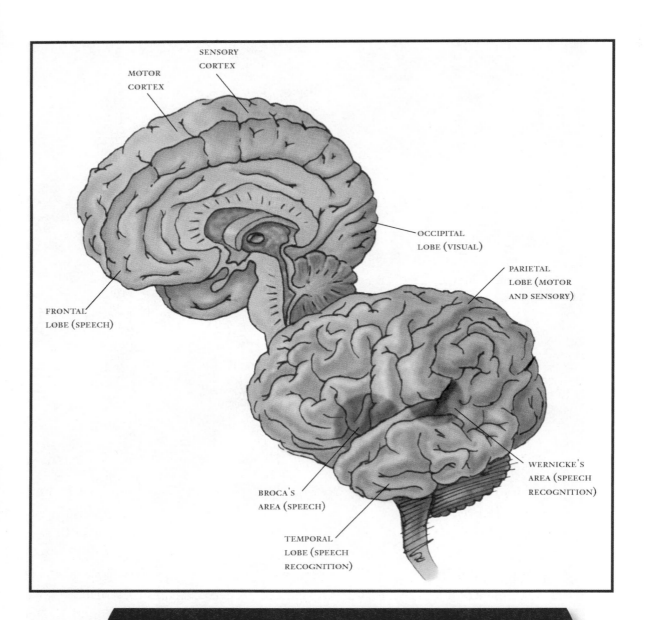

MOTOR
CORTEX

SENSORY
CORTEX

OCCIPITAL
LOBE (VISUAL)

PARIETAL
LOBE (MOTOR
AND SENSORY)

FRONTAL
LOBE (SPEECH)

WERNICKE'S
AREA (SPEECH
RECOGNITION)

BROCA'S
AREA (SPEECH)

TEMPORAL
LOBE (SPEECH
RECOGNITION)

What is so remarkable about Phineas Gage's injury is not only where the rod went in his head but where it did *not* go. The tamping iron missed a number of key areas on either side of the brain that control important functions, including Broca's and Wernicke's area, plus the motor strip and the somatosensory strip.

Humans have always argued about what makes us human. Is it our ability to walk on two feet? To hold tools in our hands? To speak and hear language? To worship a supreme being? The case of Phineas Gage suggests that we are human because our frontal lobes are set up so we can get along with other humans. We are "hard wired" to be sociable. When we lose that ability, we end up like Phineas. His closest companion was an iron rod.

Phineas Gage

Look closely to read the inscription on the famous iron: "This is the bar that was shot through the head of Mr. Phineas Gage at Cavendish, Vermont, Sept. 14, 1848. He fully recovered from the injury and deposited this bar in the museum of the Medical College of Harvard University." Someone— either Dr. Harlow or the engraver—got the date wrong. The accident was on September 13, not 14.

The tamping iron and skull of Phineas have a new home at Harvard Medical School in Boston. After 150 years on display just outside the dean's office in the medical school, they were cleaned up and moved in 2000 to a new exhibit case in the Countway Library of Medicine just down Shattuck Street. If you want to see Phineas, you have to ask permission at the library's front desk, but generally they will send you straight up to the fifth floor, where Phineas resides in Harvard's collection of medical curiosities.

The Harvard curators say that other museums, such as the Smithsonian Institution, are constantly asking to borrow Phineas's skull and iron, but his traveling days are over. The last time he was lent for exhibit in 1998, he came back with a loosened tooth. That year, Phineas went in the back seat of a limousine to Cavendish, Vermont, for a festival and medical seminar to mark the 150th anniversary of his terrible accident. Psychologists, surgeons, and neurologists came from all over the world to present scientific papers on frontal cortex injuries. Also on hand were men and women in wheelchairs who suffer from cortex injury or disease. To these special attendees, Phineas was no specimen or historical curiosity. He was a fellow sufferer.

At the end of the celebration, the town unveiled a boulder of Vermont granite on the village green with a bronze plaque as a permanent memorial to Phineas. If you go to Vermont, you can read it yourself. It explains what happened in Cavendish, what happened to Phineas, and what happened to Dr. Harlow. It explains what happened to our knowledge of the brain as a result.

In 1998, one hundred and fifty years after his terrible accident, the town of Cavendish, Vermont, held a medical seminar and festival to honor Phineas Gage. The climax was the dedication of a memorial plaque explaining what had happened to Phineas and to brain science as a result.

This Concord stagecoach ended up in a museum in Los Angeles, California, far from the New Hampshire factory where it was made. Phineas Gage ended his days in San Francisco, far from New Hampshire, where he was born; far from Vermont, where he was injured; and far from Chile, where he drove a Concord stagecoach like this one.

The plaque does not answer the question of Phineas's luck. I said at the beginning that you could decide for yourself what kind of luck he had at the end. This is what I think: Phineas Gage was lucky. His accident was terrible. It changed him into someone else, and yet Phineas figured out how to live as that new person for eleven years. He was limited in ways that are important to all human beings, but he found a way to live, working with horses. He took care of himself. He saw the world. He died with his family around him, the only people who knew both the old and new Phineas. And he drove a six-horse stagecoach. I bet Phineas Gage drove fast.

The Surgery Story

By Aidan Chang

From cave paintings to heart transplants:
A brief look at the fascinating history of surgery

▶ **8000 b.c.**
As evidenced by cave paintings and holes found in skulls, prehistoric humans may have drilled or scraped into the skull to relieve pressure on the brain or to deal with other diseases

◀ **2500 b.c.**
Ancient Egyptians performed amputations, attempted to mend broken bones, and performed dental surgery.

2000 b.c.
Hindu practices in ancient India involved removal of tumors and infected tonsils and even the first plastic surgery, using excess skin from the forehead to create new noses and ears for punished criminals.

A.D. 500–1400
In the Middle Ages, surgery was considered a lesser form of medicine. Barber-surgeons traveled from place to place to cut hair, remove tumors, stitch up wounds, pull teeth, and perform bloodlettings—procedures thought to drain the body of the sickness within.

▶ **a.d. 1600–1900**
Ambroise Paré introduced ligature, or tying off, of arteries to prevent blood loss. Ether and chloroform were used by American dentist William Morton in 1846, revolutionizing surgery by allowing

surgeons to operate without causing the patient pain. And in 1865, British surgeon Joseph Lister reduced instances of deadly infection by using phenol during surgery, having surgeons wash their hands, and sterilizing equipment.

◀ **a.d. 1900–2000**
As issues regarding infection, anesthetic, and blood were addressed, surgery took giant leaps forward with kidney and heart transplants, laser eye surgery, and robotic surgeries. Minimally invasive procedures involve the use of remote controls that guide tiny devices inserted in small incisions to repair injury or address disease. These procedures drastically lessen pain and also reduce recovery time.

Extension Activity

Connecting with a Character: Dr. Harlow took quite an interest in Phineas Gage. (a) Describe Dr. Harlow, and discuss two reasons why he was so interested in Phineas Gage. (b) Think of someone you find interesting. Describe this person and two reasons why this person is so interesting to you. (c) Write a summary of your paper.

Paper Requirements: Paper must begin with a title page that lists the paper's title, your name, and the date. Paper must be two or three pages long (not including the title page).

Also By The Author

If you enjoyed *Phineas Gage,* you may enjoy these other books authored or coauthored by John Fleischman:

- *Black and White Airmen: Their True History* (nonfiction; the story of how classmates—once separated by segregation—became World War II pilots and later friends)
- *Free & Public: One Hundred and Fifty Years at the Public Library of Cincinnati and Hamilton County,* 1853–2003 (nonfiction; the story of how the Cincinnati library became a model for libraries nationwide)
- *Mid-Century City: Cincinnati at the Apex* (nonfiction; photography by Sarge Marsh)
- *The Ohio Lands* (nonfiction; coauthored by Ian Adams; a photographic journey that celebrates the geography, history, and human-made landscapes of Ohio)

Related Topics

If you enjoyed the topics discussed in *Phineas Gage,* you may enjoy these other books that explore similar topics:

- *Black Pioneers of Science and Invention* by Louis Haber (nonfiction; account of fourteen talented African American scientists)
- *Extraordinary Women of Medicine* by Darlene R. Stille (nonfiction; stories about women who altered the history of medicine)
- *Louis Pasteur and the Hidden World of Microbes* by Louise E. Robbins (nonfiction; a scientific biography of Pasteur, focusing on the risks he took to study microbes and the implications of those studies)
- *The Teen Brain Book: Who and What Are You?* by Dale Carlson (nonfiction; a guide discussing how the brain works and how people can use their brains to rewire themselves and their habits)

HATCHET CAFE

SURVIVAL FOOD

Stuck in the wilderness? Food nowhere in sight? Stomach empty to the point of pain? Welcome to Hatchet Cafe! Below you'll find mouthwatering concoctions of wilderness wonders ready to tickle your taste buds and fill that aching tummy. Hatchet Cafe's owner, Brian, has a special place in his heart for these foods, and he's always happy to cook his customers something good to eat.

APPETIZERS

ORANGE DRINK $2.75
Sweet and tangy—almost too sweet—but so good you'll want to hold the taste on your tongue for days.

POACHED TURTLE EGGS $5.99
Our owner, Brian, prefers these straight from the shell, but most people like their eggs a little more cooked. Four eggs, perfectly poached, served with a side of wild greens.

ENTREES

WILDERNESS PB&J $6.99
You've never had a peanut-butter-and-jelly sandwich quite like this. Our jelly is made from just-picked choke cherries, and the "peanut butter" from hazelnuts.

HAZELNUT RABBIT $16.99
For those who prefer rabbit to foolbirds, try this meal of rabbit meat, fire-roasted until golden brown, topped with a hazelnut sauce.

NEW! BEEF AND POTATOES $15.99
Just in! The aroma of garlic, our special spices, and juicy beef will remind you of good, old-fashioned comfort food. Served with mashed potatoes.

FIRST MEAT $14.99
Roasted over a fire until crispy on the outside and tender on the inside, our signature "foolbirds"—or ruffed grouse—will delight you with their rich flavor.

ENTREES

BLUEGILL, SUNFISH, AND PERCH STEW $9.99
First we turn the fish over a fire until the skin crackles. The flaky, moist, and tender meat from three types of fish are then tossed together in a lake-water broth.

DESSERTS

FRESH RASPBERRIES $4.99
Straight to your table from our bushes outside the kitchen. You've never tasted anything so sweet. You might even want to drink the tangy juice from your bowl.

NEW! PEACH WHIP $5.99
Not even Brian will talk much about this dessert. His secret recipe is kept far from prying eyes. Expect something light, airy, and altogether scrumptious.

BEVERAGES

CRYSTAL LAKE WATER $1.00
Taken directly from the lake you see from our windows, this water is the cleanest, purest freshwater around. Served in a bamboo cup.

Extension Activity

Connecting with a Character: Brian learned many things during his ordeal in the wilderness. (a) Describe Brian, and discuss two things he learned as he struggled to survive. (b) Think of someone you know who has overcome a difficult situation in his or her life. Describe this person and two reasons why this person has impressed you. (c) Write a summary of your paper.

Paper Requirements: Paper must begin with a title page that lists the paper's title, your name, and the date. Paper must be two or three pages long (not including the title page).

Also By The Author

If you enjoyed *Hatchet,* you may enjoy these other books authored or coauthored by Gary Paulsen:

- *Brian's Winter* (fiction; the story of what would have happened to Brian, the main character in *Hatchet,* if he had not been rescued)
- *Guts: The True Stories Behind* Hatchet *and the Brian Books* (nonfiction; essays from Paulsen explaining the nonfiction inspirations for his fiction books)
- *The River* (fiction; the sequel to *Hatchet*)
- *Sisters/Hermanas* (fiction, with Spanish translation for bilingual readers; the tale of two girls from very different backgrounds who share an obsession with beauty)

Related Topics

If you enjoyed the topics discussed in *Hatchet,* you may enjoy these other books that explore similar topics:

- *The Divorce Express* by Paula Danziger (fiction; about a girl coping with her divorced parents and her new life)
- *Generation Green: The Ultimate Teen Guide to Living an Eco-Friendly Life* by Linda Sivertsen and Tosh Sivertsen (nonfiction; a guide for teens who want to become more eco-savvy)
- *It's Disgusting and We Ate It! True Food Facts from Around the World and Throughout History* by James Solheim (nonfiction; a humorous report on bizarre foods around the world, including interesting and fun facts)
- *Lizard Island* by Sneed B. Collard (nonfiction; about Lizard Island, where scientists are studying the Great Barrier Reef)

Glossary

A

abscess
A swollen pocket in tissue where dead bacteria and immune cells collect during an infection. (p. 151)

accommodation
Change made to increase convenience; traveling space. (pp. 10; 116)

achromatopsia
An eye disorder affecting the ability to see colors. (p. 16)

adamant
Not able to be swayed. (p. 8)

anticonvulsant
A drug that prevents or reduces seizures. (p. 180)

anti–inflammatory
Something that reduces swelling. (p. 30)

aphasia
The inability to speak. (p. 182)

apparatus
Equipment used for a particular purpose. (p. 15)

austral
Related to the south. (pp. 63, 76)

autobiography
A story a person writes about his or her life. (p. 133)

B

bacteria
Simple, one–celled organisms that can produce many new generations in a short time, such as *E. coli*. (p. 150)

barren
To be without plant life. (p. 63)

barrier
An object that stops the movement of another object. (p. 30)

base
A camp or main place to work. (pp. 63, 66, 69, 76, 85)

beckon
To signal something to come toward you. (p. 71)

benevolence
Kindness. (pp. 168, 172)

bolster
To support or strengthen. (p. 14)

bootie
A sock for a dog to protect from ice forming between its toes; a shoe cover used by doctors and nurses to keep germs from spreading. (pp. 11, 27, 35, 36; 158)

Braille
A system of writing, for people who are blind, consisting of raised dots. (p. 12)

brain stem
The bottom part of the brain that links to the spinal cord and controls such involuntary functions as breathing, heart rate, and reflex reactions. (pp. 160, 161, 163–164, 170, 193)

brawl
A fight. (p. 50)

brushbow
A curved piece in front of the main body of a sled designed to protect the sled from brush. (p. 28)

bulletproof
Not easily damaged. (p. 26)

Glossary

C

cadaver
A dead body, often used for dissection. (p. 160)

carbolic acid
A strong, corrosive chemical poison once used as a disinfectant. (p. 151)

careen
To move quickly in an out-of-control way. (p. 25)

caustic
Very unkind. (p. 19)

cerebellum
The part of the brain that coordinates movement. (pp. 160, 161, 164, 167, 170)

cesarean section
A procedure in which a baby is born by means of surgery. (p. 7)

charade
Something so fake that few people are fooled. (p. 12)

checkpoint
An official stopping place. (pp. 26, 29–31, 34, 35, 39, 40)

chute
A passage through which things go. (pp. 27, 28)

circumnavigate
To complete a circular route. (p. 101)

claustrophobic
Afraid of being in small places. (p. 14)

clique
A small group of people who don't want other people included. (p. 19)

cognitive
Related to thinking. (p. 12)

complexion
The appearance of the skin on a person's face. (p. 63)

conceive
To imagine. (p. 88)

congenital
A condition present since birth. (pp. 11, 16)

conquer
To defeat. (p. 74)

conscience
A feeling that tells a person something is right or wrong. (pp. 20, 40, 67)

conservative
Very cautious. (p. 30)

conservator
A person who protects or restores something. (p. 127)

continent
A very large area of land. (pp. 49, 51–53, 66, 74, 76, 79, 98)

corpus callosum
A bundle of neurons in the brain that connects the left and right hemispheres of the cortex. (pp. 162, 163, 170)

courteous
Describes a person who has good manners and is polite to other people. (p. 124)

crevasse
A deep crack in the ground. (pp. 56, 70, 71)

curious
Strange or unusual. (p. 52)

current
The movement of water in a certain direction. (p. 79)

Glossary

D

daguerreotype
A process for taking pictures using a metal plate. (p. 158)

demeanor
Behavior; appearance. (p. 20)

depot
A storage place for supplies. (pp. 71, 76)

derrick
A crane for lifting heavy objects. (p. 146)

destination
A place someone is going. (p. 76)

deteriorating
Worsening. (p. 38)

deviant
Different in a bad way. (p. 19)

discourse
Conversation. (p. 8)

disintegrate
To break up into smaller pieces. (p. 86)

dispirited
Sad and having no hope. (p. 101)

E

ecstatic
Very happy. (p. 28)

electroencephalograph (EEG)
A procedure that traces electrical patterns in the brain. (p. 168)

electronically
Describes something that is done using a computer. (pp. 191, 193)

emanate
To come out. (p. 25)

emetic
Something that causes a person to vomit. (p. 153)

endurance
The ability to remain strong in tough conditions. (pp. 74, 101)

epidemic
A disease that spreads quickly to many people. (p. 106)

ether
A class of organic compounds; once used as anesthesia during operations, but proven to be dangerous for patients. (pp. 158, 159)

exhilaration
A feeling of being very happy and excited. (p. 25)

exhume
To dig up a corpse from a grave. (p. 185)

exotic
Unusual. (p. 64)

expedition
A journey of exploration. (pp. 47, 49, 52–54, 57, 58, 63, 64, 66, 67, 69, 71, 73–75, 88, 98)

eyewitness
Somebody who saw an event and can testify to what happened. (pp. 123, 124, 157, 160)

F

farsightedness
A condition that occurs when the shape of the eye is too short; a person who is farsighted has trouble seeing things that are close but can easily see images that are farther away. (p. 16)

Glossary

fatigue
Extreme tiredness. (pp. 34, 37)

ferocity
Wildness; cruelty. (p. 101)

fetch
To bring back. (p. 96)

fissure
A crack. (p. 10)

flank
A side of something. (p. 53)

floe
A large, flat piece of ice. (pp. 53, 76, 83, 85, 86, 88)

forbidding
Not inviting (p. 51)

foul
Disgusting. (p. 53)

frigid
Very cold. (pp. 51, 54, 81, 86)

frontal lobe
The part of the cortex at the front of the brain. (pp. 146, 182, 184, 191, 194, 196)

frontier
Wilderness. (p. 52)

G

gale
A very strong wind. (pp. 56, 90, 98)

gangline
The main line that connects the dogs to the sled. (pp. 28, 31)

gangrene
A life-threatening condition occurring when infection and lack of circulation causes tissue to die. (p. 150)

garment
A piece of clothing. (p. 47)

gash
A large, deep cut. (p. 79)

genealogy
The study of the history of families over several generations. (p. 12)

genetics
The study of how characteristics such as eye color are passed from one generation to the next. (p. 11)

glacial
Formed by a glacier. (p. 54)

gnaw
To cause worry. (p. 71)

H

hallucinate
To see, feel, or hear something that is not really there. (pp. 34, 37, 38)

handler
A person who assists the person driving a dogsled. (p. 28)

hereditary
Characteristics passed by parents to their children before birth. (p. 11)

Hike!
Dogsled command signaling the dogs to move forward. (p. 24)

hoist
To lift. (p. 81)

humiliation
A strong feeling of embarrassment. (p. 61)

hurl
To throw something with force. (p. 86)

Glossary

hypothermia
A serious medical condition in which body temperature becomes very low. (pp. 33, 181)

hypothetical
Describes an idea or theory that is not proven. (p. 192)

I

Iditarod
A difficult sled-dog race of more than 1,150 miles from Anchorage to Nome, Alaska. (pp. 7, 13, 22–28, 30–35, 39–41)

impersonate
To act like somebody else. (p. 80)

indiscreet
Unreasonable; uncontrolled. (p. 23)

inflammation
Swelling, redness, and pain in an area of the body as a reaction to injury or infection. (p. 151)

inlet
A narrow area of water leading from an ocean into land. (p. 66)

intrigue
A complicated plot. (p. 101)

investment
Something that will increase in worth later. (p. 64)

J

journalism
A job that requires writing news stories for TV, radio, magazines, or newspapers. (p. 64)

K

knight
An honorary British title; to give someone the title of a knight. (pp. 69; 72)

L

labor
To make physical effort. (p. 93)

languid
Slow and weak. (p. 37)

legally blind
A person sees at twenty feet what someone else with perfect eyesight can see at two hundred feet. (pp. 9, 10, 12)

lumber
To move in a slow and awkward way. (p. 181)

M

microorganism
A living thing that is so small that it can be seen only through a microscope. (pp. 150, 151)

mill
To move around without a particular purpose. (p. 35)

monotony
Something that is boring. (p. 32)

musher
A person who drives a dogsled. (pp. 10, 13, 26–29, 31, 32, 34, 37, 40, 41)

Glossary

N

nearsightedness
A condition that occurs when the shape of the eye is too long; a person who is nearsighted can see things that are close but cannot make out things far away. (p. 16)

neuron
A nerve cell that transmits electrical or chemical impulses. (pp. 163, 165–167, 172)

O

occipital lobe
The part of the cortex at the back of the head. (pp. 163, 164)

ophthalmologist
A doctor who treats eye disorders. (p. 9)

oppressive
Overwhelming. (p. 15)

optimism
The belief that good things will happen. (p. 101)

ordeal
A difficult experience. (pp. 63, 93)

ostracize
To not include someone. (p. 19)

outcropping
A rock sticking out of the ground. (p. 57)

outlandish
Unusual or strange. (p. 21)

P

panorama
A view you can see over a wide area of land. (p. 10)

parch
To make very thirsty. (p. 93)

parietal lobe
The middle portion of the cortex at the top of the head. (pp. 163, 164)

Parliament
The lawmaking body in Great Britain. (p. 64)

pathetic
Sad; sorrowful. (p. 90)

pediatric
Related to the practice of medicine dealing with children. (p. 7)

penicillin
The first widely used antibiotic. (p. 151)

perplexing
Confusing. (p. 34)

perverse
Something that is the opposite of what is right. (p. 20)

philoprogenitiveness
Parental love. (p. 168)

pitiful
Sad; sorrowful. (p. 83)

placate
To calm in order to stop one from feeling angry. (p. 8)

plague
To cause problems. (p. 98)

plume
A small cloud. (p. 53)

Glossary

profusely
To a great extent. (p. 36)

psychologist
A person who studies human behavior. (pp. 176, 197)

Q

quagmire
An area of soft, wet, muddy ground. (p. 32)

qualification
A skill or characteristic that makes a person capable of doing an activity or task. (p. 121)

quarantine
To keep sick people away from others. (p. 107)

R

receptive aphasia
The inability to understand speech. (p. 182)

rejuvenated
Strong again. (p. 32)

reluctantly
Not wanting to do something. (p. 66)

reputation
The opinion people have of others based on what has happened in the past. (p. 120)

resolve
A strong determination. (p. 23)

retaliation
Harming someone who has harmed you. (p. 21)

retinal
Relating to part of the eye at the back of the eyeball. (p. 11)

rigging
Gear, such as ropes, used on a ship. (p. 50)

routine
A fixed way of doing something. (p. 64)

runner
A narrow ski on the bottom of a dogsled that the person stands on. (pp. 24, 25, 28, 32–34)

S

seam
A line made when two flat objects are joined. (p. 81)

seethe
To be very angry; to foam, like seawater. (pp. 20; 90)

seizure
A sudden, involuntary contraction of the muscles usually caused by a disruption of the normal electrical patterns of the brain. (p. 181)

selfless
Caring about others more than you care about yourself. (p. 101)

sepsis
A severe bacterial infection. (p. 150)

shaly
Covered with shale, a type of rock. (p. 53)

sheer
Unmixed with other things. (p. 58)

shriek
To make a high-pitched noise. (p. 93)

Glossary

smorgasbord
A meal with many kinds of foods. (p. 39)

snow hook
A large metal hook attached to a dogsled; can be driven into snow to hold the sled steady. (pp. 29, 33)

solemn
Very serious. (pp. 21, 107)

solitude
The state of being alone. (p. 50)

soul search
A careful examination of thoughts and feelings to make a decision. (p. 39)

spectrum
A range of different colors. (p. 15)

spinal cord
The cables carrying the nerves from the brain stem to the rest of the body. (pp. 160, 163, 165, 167, 170)

square–rigger
A type of sailing ship. (p. 50)

stamina
Physical strength to do something for a long time. (p. 38)

straggle
To wander. (p. 94)

straggler
One who fell behind. (p. 38)

streptococci
A type of bacteria that cause disease. (pp. 150, 152)

stupendous
Very large and impressive. (p. 70)

suffrage
The right to vote. (pp. 131, 135)

summit
To climb to the highest point; the highest point. (pp. 35; 69)

synapse
The tiny space between neurons. (pp. 165, 166)

synonymous
Having the same meaning. (p. 101)

T

tamp
To pack something down. (pp. 145–147, 194)

tandem sled
A dogsled designed for two people. (pp. 23, 24)

tedious
Boring. (pp. 64, 69)

temporal lobe
The part of the cortex on the side of the head. (pp. 163, 164, 182, 184, 196)

treacherous
Dangerous. (p. 88)

tugline
A line that connects a dog's harness to the gangline. (pp. 30, 35)

U

unconstitutional
Not allowed by the rules of a country. (p. 116)

uninhabited
Without people. (pp. 88, 89)

unscathed
Not hurt. (p. 86)

Glossary

V

vast
Very large. (pp. 70, 71, 88)

veneer
An object's exterior coating. (p. 96)

vessel
A ship. (p. 66)

vigilance
The state of being alert and watchful of danger. (p. 129)

vise
A tool that holds an object firmly in place. (p. 81)

vivid
Very detailed. (p. 50)

vulnerable
Easily hurt. (p. 14)

W

welfare
One's comfort and well-being. (p. 13)

whiteout
A polar weather condition with heavy snow that makes vision difficult. (p. 61)

wick
To pull liquid away. (p. 34)

Index

Index

Index

K

knight, 69, 72

L

labor, 93
languid, 37
legally blind, 9, 10, 12
Lewis family, 114, 115
localization, 172, 182
lumber, 181

M

MacMillan, Professor
  Malcolm, 176, 177
Marshall, Eric, 69, 71, 72
Masons, 110–112
Massachusetts, 158,
  184–186
McDowell, Calvin,
  121–124, 135
McKee, Sandy, 36
McMurdo Sound, 54, 57,
  63, 66, 67, 69, 72, 98
*Memphis Diary of Ida B.
  Wells,* 133, 138–139
*Memphis Free Speech and
  Headlight,* 120, 123, 125,
  135
Memphis, Tennessee, 106,
  115, 118–126, 133, 135
microorganism, 150, 151
mill, 35
Mississippi, 105, 114, 123,
  124, 135
monotony, 32
Moss, Maurine, 121, 122

Moss, Thomas, 121–124,
  135
Moss, Thomas, Jr., 122
Mount Erebus, 53, 69

N

nearsightedness, 16
neurotransmitter, 165–167
New England, 170, 175–177
New Hampshire, 149, 153,
  155, 177–179, 199
New York, New York,
  125, 126, 175–177
New York Age, 125–127
Nightingale, Taylor, 120,
  121
Nimrod (ship), 66, 67, 69,
  72

O

Oklahoma, 124
ophthalmologist, 9
oppressive, 15
optimism, 101
ordeal, 63, 93
ostracize, 19
outcropping, 57
outlandish, 21

P

panorama, 10
parch, 93
Parliament, 64
pathetic, 90
Patten, John, 13
pediatric, 7
perplexing, 34

perverse, 20
petitioned, 129
philoprogenitiveness, 168
phrenology, 168–172, 182
pitiful, 83
placate, 8
plague, 98
plight, 130
plume, 53
profusely, 36
psychologist, 176, 197
purgative, 153

Q

quagmire, 32
qualification, 121
quarantine, 107
Quest (ship), 98–100

R

realization, 133
rejuvenated, 32
reluctantly, 66
reputation, 120
resolve, 23
retaliation, 21
retinal, 11
Riddles, Libby, 7, 26, 28
rigging, 50
Ross Ice Shelf, 53, 55, 66
routine, 64
Rowan, Jay, 38, 41
Royal Geographical
  Society, 51, 54, 64

Index

Photo Credits